WITH
JESUS
IN THE
WORLD

To my father, Willard,
who like Abraham looked for a better country and, in a
lifetime of being a pilgrim and stranger, represented the
kingdom of God in new and distant places.

To all missionaries
who, for the sake of the gospel, have returned to Ur.

WITH JESUS

IN THE
WORLD

Mission in Modern Affluent Societies

Linford Stutzman
Foreword by Wilbert Shenk

HERALD PRESS
Scottdale, Pennsylvania
Waterloo, Ontario

Library of Congress Cataloging-in-Publication Data
Stutzman, Linford, 1950-
    With Jesus in the world : mission in modern affluent societies /
Linford Stutzman.
        p.   cm.
    Includes bibliographical references.
    ISBN 0-8361-3599-7 (alk. paper)
    1. Missions—Sociological aspects.   2. Wealth—Religious
aspects—Christianity.   3. Anabaptists.   I. Title.
BV2063.S88   1992
266'.001—dc20   92-16599
                                                                          CIP

The paper used in this publication is recycled and meets the mini-
mum requirements of American National Standard for Information Sciences—Permanence of Paper for Printed Library Materials,
ANSI Z39.48-1984.

00 99 98 97 96 95 94 93 92 9 8 7 6 5 4 3 2 1

Contents

List of Charts

Foreword

Modern culture originated in the Enlightenment, that movement of the sixteenth and seventeenth centuries which dealt with the world and knowledge through science and scientific technology. Modern societies are those that have modernized their economies through sustained application of technology. A century ago 75 percent of workers in Europe and North America were employed in food production. Today a mere 3 percent of the work force produces far more food than was possible using traditional methods. Modern society is industrialized and urbanized.

The transition from traditional to modern society took place in the West in a few generations; the basic course was already set by the mid-nineteenth century. The shift from rural to urban created a new society. Although the individual lived with many more people, relations changed. It was no longer possible to know everyone in the "village."

With the introduction of mass production techniques, the nature of work was fundamentally altered. Science became the arbiter of human knowledge. Scientism promoted the view that religion was incompatible with science because science was based on fact while religion was superstition.

The church in modern society has been on the defensive

and thus at a disadvantage. But this disadvantage has been compounded by another fact. The church in the West was rooted in Christendom; it had no mission other than political and cultural conformity and protection of the status quo.

As we come to the end of the twentieth century, we are seeing a groundswell of concern for Christian witness in modern affluent societies. Modern culture has marginalized the church; participation in the church continues to decline. Yet modern society is filled with religion. For example, observers have noted the religious dimensions of the modern shopping mall. It functions as a lavish temple of the god Mammon, its very layout replete with religious symbolism.

This is a moment of great opportunity as well as risk. If the church can recover its true nature as a missionary community, it can make an impact on modern society. But the church risks yielding to marketing experts who see it as another competitor for the public's money, time, and interest.

Linford Stutzman's study challenges—indeed, inspires—with its vision of missionary witness based on Jesus' example. Stutzman roots his thesis in actual experiences of Mennonite mission initiatives in Dublin, London, Munich, Hong Kong, and Tokyo—all set in modern societies. Stutzman knows this milieu at firsthand because of his own years of missionary experience in Germany and Australia.

How, asks Stutzman, can we represent Jesus Christ and the reign of God in modern societies with the same effect Jesus had in Palestine or an Anabaptist Hans Hut had in Europe? Through a gospel, Stutzman answers, which offers God's *shalom* to counteract the dehumanizing effects of modern culture. Stutzman calls for going beyond conventional mission strategies to a more radical and biblical approach, which he discerns in the incarnation of Jesus.

Key to understanding the incarnation is the notion of social location. Today many congregations are trapped by their social location, their witness neutralized by what they "owe" their particular socio-economic class. The originality of Stutzman's approach is to suggest that in his incarnation Jesus used his social location as a springboard for witness to the whole of society. This is the model the missionary church should seek to follow in modern affluent society.

> —*Wilbert R. Shenk, Mission Training Center*
> *Associated Mennonite Biblical Seminaries*
> *Elkhart, Indiana*

Preface

From 1978 to 1986, my wife, Janet, and I lived in Munich, West Germany—one of the most successful, modern, affluent cities on earth. We were there as Mennonite missionaries. Our goal was to establish a new congregation, a free church in the Anabaptist tradition, among the secular and sophisticated urbanites of that city. When we left Munich, after eight years of intense activity, we left behind a healthy, growing congregation of thirty members.

In 1527 there slipped into Munich an unknown missionary. He belonged to the Anabaptist movement—that left wing of the Protestant Reformation which was just beginning to sweep southern, German-speaking Europe with the radically new concept of voluntary church membership. Within just three days, a small congregation of around thirty members had been established. Some of those who joined the new church were martyred shortly thereafter. It seems that this unknown Anabaptist missionary accomplished in a matter of weeks what it took us eight years to accomplish in Munich 460 years later—this despite the threat of martyrdom.

Why the glaring difference in effectiveness between those efforts and our modern ones? Both efforts were rooted in the same tradition and took place in the same city. What had changed in the meantime? Are modern urbanites simply less interested in faith than were their ancestors? Have the apparent successes of modern society made discipleship and the costs of faith seem comparatively unattractive? Could it be that missionaries have changed, or are now seen to be irrelevant? Are missionaries preaching the same message?

We had, along with many of our mission colleagues in Europe, often pointed to statistics indicating Europe's incredibly low receptivity to the gospel as presented by evangelical missionaries. This served as an excuse for the apparent ineffectiveness of our witness. "Europe, with its modern history of secularism, humanistic ideologies, and affluence, is the hardest mission field in the world today," we would tell each other. It made us feel only a little better.

But how helpful to our mission endeavor is it to point to apparent vast differences between society today and the society of the Reformation and Anabaptist movement? By emphasizing the differences, do we risk reducing the dynamic Anabaptist movement from a normative model for missions to an interesting historical chapter of church history?

Society has changed in Germany, as in all affluent countries, during the past five centuries. But which changes make the preaching of the gospel so ineffective? Is it helpful to identify such social changes as rationalism, affluence, urbanization, and technology as being the obstacles to church development?

Or is the problem not so much that society has changed but that the church and the missionaries who are sent have changed in relation to society? Do the evangelical churches of North America and the missionaries it sends have a position within society fundamentally different from that of the evangelists of the early Anabaptist movement? Might this social shift lie at the root of the contrasts?

These questions, lurking in the long shadow of that unknown, effective Anabaptist missionary in Munich nearly 500 years earlier, were constantly with us during our eight years there. This shadow and the accompanying questions reached us all the way in Perth, Western Australia. There we served in church development in a city whose inhabitants (although on the other side of the world from Munich) share the characteristics of modern affluent urbanites everywhere—high incomes and low church involvement.

This book has grown out of an ongoing struggle with practical missiological questions. It reflects ideas developed through study and practice. The most significant contributions, however, were relationships with persons with whom I worked. Also crucial were the intense, often late-night discussions with people of commitment and dissimilar kinds of faith: atheists, artists, hedonists, fellow missionaries, Marxists, social activists, and pietists.

There were people like Siegfried Thaler of Munich, whom I met as a young law student, and who, as a humanist, was deeply committed to pacifism. Another was Josef Berthold, also of Munich, a street musician and social activist. Both came to faith, then on the road of discipleship experienced a transformation of their activism. Their intellectual and spiritual depth, especially their ability to recognize missionary hypocrisy, continue to make me honest.

In Perth, I learned much from members of the faculty at the Baptist Theological College of Western Australia who are committed both to radical discipleship and to integrity in mission. Wes Hartley, minister in the Uniting Church of Australia, and his wife, Jan, taught us much about commitment to relevance and the high cost of faithfulness. The support and inspiration of my colleagues of the Western Australian Association for Urban Mission was invaluable. They modeled interdenominational cooperation and integration of word and deed.

Having served for twelve years with Eastern Mennonite Board of Missions and Charities, I wish to give special thanks to the board for its encouragement. I am grateful for the board's extension to us of freedom to experiment and even fail in our attempts to apply this book's principles in mission.

A special thanks to my wife Janet, who has shared the stresses and blessings, successes and failures of mission life. Thanks also to sons David and Jonathan, for sharing Janet's support and for giving up computer game time so that I could work on this.

A note of explanation is necessary. Having been involved in mission in modern affluent societies, I include myself when referring positively—and negatively—to missionaries. I have made the mistakes of missionaries. I have tried also to practice what I preach.

Further, as a Mennonite I look to the Anabaptist movement, not only as the roots of my denomination, but also as a relevant model for missions in general. It is my hope that missionaries and church planters from many traditions will find this book helpful in our common task of sharing the good news in good societies.

—*Linford Stutzman*
Harrisonburg, Virginia

Introduction

The Central Issue:
The Sociology of the Incarnation

It is impossible to address the resistance to the gospel in modern affluent societies without examining the relationship and social position of the evangelist as well as of the developing evangelistic church within society. Traditional churches, North American evangelical missionaries, and the churches they develop all bear witness, through their social relationships, to God's character and relationship to humanity.

Jürgen Moltmann writes,

> Before anyone says a single word in the church, the church itself has already spoken. It has spoken through the form it takes in society. . . . The Church's social and political form and its cultural tradition are a continual witness. The only question is: a witness to what and a witness to whom? . . . The church always belongs within the context of the world, whether it likes it or not.[1]

Missionaries may not feel they are *of* the world. But sociologically they are as much *in* the world as all other people in that society. Furthermore, in modern affluent societies, most people (missionaries included) have much freedom to choose how they fit into the society and which persons in the society they will relate to. With whom do we missionaries identify in society? Do we deliberately choose our place or location within society? If so, where?

For Jesus it was not identification with humankind in general that shaped the nature of his ministry. It was, rather, the deliberate identification with a certain part of society that determined how his ministry was perceived. The impact of his words, how the good news of the kingdom was communicated, to whom it appealed, and to whom it sounded threatening—all were affected by Jesus' place in society. Jesus did not "bloom where he was planted" by accident. He was "planted" deliberately.

The social location of the Anabaptists in sixteenth-century European society also could be seen as having crucial impact on the message, method, and impact of the movement's evangelists during the early years. In a later chapter we will examine more closely the missiological implications of the early Anabaptist social location.

The social location of the missionary and the emerging church in modern societies will be seen, then, as the key missiological issue in this study. It is assumed that the location within society which the missionary and the developing church have either chosen or accepted is crucial. Location shapes, in central ways, the method of proclaiming the good news as well as the content of the message. Location ultimately determines the impact of the mission endeavor on the whole of society.

Missionaries who are beginning to work in affluent societies must do so by deliberately and carefully choosing the social location of their witness. To be at once effective and faithful to the model of Jesus, the Christian fellowship which emerges must begin in the right place.

In approaching the missiological questions of missionaries in modern affluent societies according to such assumptions, the model of Jesus in his society, as well as of the Anabaptists in theirs, can be helpful. In this way the incarnation can be our model of witness in Germany as well as Galilee, in Japan as well as Judea, in Pittsburgh as well as Palestine.

This study will address the issues of the relative ineffectiveness of missions in affluent societies by looking first at modern society, then at the position and identity within society of the witnesses of the kingdom of God.

We will begin with Jesus. Then we will look at the early Anabaptist movement. Finally we will examine several modern mission efforts and the resultant emerging churches in several representative cities. The final chapter will deal with possible practical applications for mission based on these models.

WITH
JESUS
IN THE
WORLD

CHAPTER 1

Modern Affluent Society and the Missionary

Modern Affluent Society

It is difficult to preach the good news of the kingdom of God in societies where the kingdoms of men and women are working so well.

The participants in the Martyrs' Synod[1] in Augsburg, Germany, in 1527 were optimistic. Although under the threat of death, they courageously planned to evangelize all Europe.

In contrast, today missionary conferences in that part of the world are called "retreats" and concentrate on missionary survival skills rather than bold evangelistic strategies. Articles by missionaries reporting of small struggling congregations in modern affluent societies rarely appear in the same issues of mission magazines offering exciting reports from developing countries.

A quick look at worldwide church statistics reveals a close correlation in most modern affluent countries between their high ranking on physical quality of life indexes and their low ranking on evangelical growth rate indexes. For instance,

take the fifteen countries that rank highest in physical quality of life out of 165 countries measured. All rank in the bottom 30 percent of the net evangelical growth rate (Japan being the one exception). Australia, which ranks fifteenth in
terms of physical quality of life, is third from the bottom of
the list of evangelical growth rate statistics, with annual
"growth" (–1.68 percent).[2]

Although affluent societies differ from one another his-
torically and culturally, the church statistics in these societies are so striking similar that Bruce Wilson, an Australian
sociologist, Anglican bishop, and student of the decline of
the Australian church, has concluded that "modern irreli-
gion is the nature of industrial society."[3]

Lesslie Newbigin maintains that modern affluent society
should not really be labeled *secular* at all. *Secular* implies neu-
trality and modern society is not neutral but is rather

> a pagan society, and its paganism, having been born out of the
> rejection of Christianity, is far more resistant to the gospel
> than the pre-Christian paganism with which cross-cultural
> missions have been familiar. Here, surely, is the most chal-
> lenging missionary frontier of our time.[4]

Orlando Costas describes our post-Christian Western
culture even more polemically as "a narcissistic culture, a
practically atheistic region which is part of a demonic capi-
talistic world."[5]

A significant amount of analysis has been done on the
philosophical, social, and psychological factors that together
create the difficulty of effectively sharing the good news of
the kingdom in modern societies. There seems to be consensus that the success of modern people in making and achieving their own goals in every area of life lies at the bottom of
secularism.[6]

In secular society, faith is an "unnecessary" option. Religion in this kind of society becomes either a private matter

divorced from present material existence, or provides a philosophical/religious basis on which an efficiently functioning modern society can be built.[7] "The dream of a world order, integrated by religion . . . had been a utopian dream long before the coming of Christ."[8] This dream, 2000 years after Christ, still appears to be alive and well in the West.

It is not the purpose of this book, however, to focus on these many complex factors. It is, rather to begin to look at the effect all this has on the missionary, the message presented, and the method by which the missionary announces the good news of the kingdom.

Lack of effectiveness is not the only problem for the missionary in this kind of society. Such a society also causes a personal problem for the missionary. The society in which the missionary lives seems, by its very character, to be prejudiced against the message with which she[9] is so closely identified. The missionary is part of a society that seems not to have a place for her. In the face of the obvious success of the modern affluent society, a society of professionals with clearly defined roles, the missionary feels small and insignificant in preaching the good news of the kingdom.

In spite of her qualifications, her commitment, her training, she does not feel very useful, for a "great division separates the church from the world which it earnestly seeks to serve."[10] What are the effects of this great division on the missionary?

The Missionary

North American missionaries who serve in modern societies are confronted with a society that seems to function at least as well, if not better, than the one from which they were sent. Few major cities of the developed world rival the desperate and dangerous social conditions obvious in Washington, D.C. The socialized medical system works far better in

Germany than does the private, inequitable health care system in the United States.

For every human problem, it seems, there is a technological or political solution that works. In this good society of peace, prosperity, and religious apathy, the missionary is supposed to witness to the good news of the kingdom. Yet even the poor seem better off financially than the missionary.

The missionary may begin to feel that, unlike the Son who left the perfection of heaven to bring the good news of God's kingdom to a very imperfect and suffering society, she has gone in the opposite direction. The words of Jesus' inaugural address in the synagogue at Nazareth, the words of fantastic hope for the poor and captive, seem feeble and irrelevant when used by the missionary in the context of upward mobility, efficiency, and power.

It is unlikely that the missionary can readily find many obviously needy people, at least ones who recognize themselves as such. Instead, the missionary finds apparently satisfied people who seem constantly to ask the missionary, "Why have you come *here*?" The missionary hears the subtle message: "*We* don't need you."

The missionary naturally wants to protect her sense of self-esteem and rationalize the lack of measurable results in her ministry to herself and the folks back home. She may thus initially seek to understand and then describe those factors in modern, affluent society that hinder the effectiveness of her witness. "Post-Christian" and "pagan" begin to creep into the missionary's vocabulary.

She may justify the lack of results in a way that is especially tempting to missionaries of denominations and churches that highly value faithfulness. This is to maintain that "those of us who do not produce so many people from our missions are probably doing it better, because we develop higher qualities in the people we win."[11]

The explaining process does help the missionary and her supporters appreciate the difficulty of the task and cope with the tensions of living and working in an unresponsive society. However, it eventually becomes apparent that coping and explaining are not the purpose of her being there. She is there to witness effectively. To do so she must in some way apply her insights to maximize her efforts in mission.

The serious missionary—that is, one who recognizes that measurable, quantitative results are indeed at least part of the missionary's goal—eventually begins to strategize. Thinking strategically is a logical and necessary response to a difficult mission situation for two reasons. First, the missionary's training has likely given her the tools with which to think strategically. The usefulness of such tools, derived from the social sciences and the advertising industry, is self-understood.

Second, the modern affluent society in which she lives focuses on efficiency, productivity, and growth in every sector. Her society is competitive, and its institutions and business organizations think strategically in their attempts to survive and expand. The primary problem of missions in modern affluent society is seen then, by both the missionary and the society in which she witnesses, to be strategic in nature.

This assertion is so obvious that it hardly seems necessary to mention. The literature of the church growth movement as well as the missiological thinking that it has influenced is thoroughly strategic in nature. Donald McGavran has written,

> An essential task is to discern receptivity and—when this is seen—to adjust methods, institutions, and personnel until the receptive are becoming Christians and reaching out to win their fellows to eternal life. Effective evangelism is demanded.[12]

The point here is that the missionary often responds to the lack of receptivity in modern society by first thinking strategically, rather than theologically. As John Howard Yoder points out,

> It is assumed that we have an adequate theology which we have received from the past. . . . We do not really need any more theological clarification. What we need now is efficiency. Our theology is basically all right.[13]

Strategic thinking, which seems to be a modern response to the modern problems of witnessing in modern society, has far reaching consequences. Strategic thinking affects everything the missionary is and does. We will first examine the effect of strategic thinking on the theological process of the missionary.

The Effects of Strategic Thinking

Market-based approaches

One way in which strategic thinking affects the theological process of the missionary in modern society is through emphasizing the individual and private rather than corporate and public dimensions of society. Strategic thinking, influenced by the secular, market-based approach, is forced in the direction of meeting individual needs, for it is the individual consumer who personally determines the nature of his or her need and selects the solution to it. Newbigin observes,

> In contrast to traditional societies, modern Western society leaves its members free, within very wide limits, to adopt and hold their own views about what is good and desirable, about what kind of life is to be admired, about what code of ethics should govern one's life.[14]

For example, in modern society many individuals have stressful lifestyles. The symptoms of stress may include painful headaches. Pain is the felt need and whole industries have been built up to develop and market products that alleviate the pain. While the advertising strategists of the companies that produce pain relievers may be fully aware that they are not offering solutions to headaches—only relief—they also know this is what the market demands.

The market, dictated by individuals with headaches, demands relief of symptoms, not help in changing personal lifestyles that cause the pain. In the end, the success of the marketing strategy is measured by the number of sales, not the reduction of headaches.

The counterpart in missions would move the strategic-thinking missionary to shape her message in response to the symptoms of personal sin rather than the deeper levels of sin itself. One example of a deeper level of sin in affluent societies is the contemporary form of pagan idolatry. As Roelf Kuitse has observed about modern society,

> Paganism remains a continuing temptation: to move away from the God of Jesus Christ to absolutized fragments of created order; to rebel against the God of grace by putting human trust in what is at the disposal of humans in the created order.[15]

While the missionary may recognize this to be true, she is also aware that there is no market for the message of exposing false gods. There is little consumer demand for the prophetical. There is, on the other hand, a huge market for products, including spiritual ones, which alleviate the debilitating side effects of individuals who worship modern idols.

In this way the message of the missionary is shaped on every level by the process of strategic thinking—from the theological foundations on which the message is built to the way the message is presented. The success of the strategic

approach is measured, as in the example of headache reme-
dies, in the number of people who choose as a remedy to
their felt needs the particular spiritual solution being offered. The impact the gospel has on the society as a whole is
not addressed.

The gospel does, of course, meet the personal, felt needs
of individuals. And beginning on the level of felt needs need
not restrict the gospel to addressing these needs. But a
problematic theological bias is created by strategic thinking.
In a process that begins with strategic thinking, a theological
shift is likely to occur that often weakens the prophetic, revolutionary character of the gospel. What is left is a message
tailored to and packaged to meet the self-diagnosed problems of individuals.

Paul Hiebert has drawn attention to this free market dimension of decision making in consumer societies in an article appropriately titled "Window Shopping for the
Gospel."[16] In modern societies there is freedom of personal
choice, and the missionary is tempted to respond to the market demands. There are distinct theological dangers in pre-
senting the gospel in ways attractive to comparative bargain-
hunting shoppers. How tempting it is for the missionary to
present the gospel as an opiate for those seeking pain-reliev-
ing spiritual drugs. This is especially true when the missionary is assured by the grateful ex-sufferer that he "feels so
good now and has looked everywhere to find a church like
this one."

Target groups

Besides the process just described, another kind of shift
occurs, of a relational or social nature. It has to do with the
unique nature of the felt needs by which individuals in affluent societies are plagued. The missionary in these societies
becomes increasingly aware that, despite apparent prosperity, stability, and success, there are many individuals with

needs readily recognized and acknowledged by those who have them. These are needs to which the gospel can potentially speak.

In thinking strategically the missionary will attempt to determine the target groups within a particular society. The aim will then be to direct the message of the gospel to those most receptive and in a way that corresponds to their felt needs. These target groups, identifiable by market-based research methods, are those in society who recognize their need and are open to solutions which will, at the very least, alleviate the symptoms. Two main types of target groups are immediately evident: the *obviously needy* and the *disguised needy*.

A word about the choice of the terms *disguised* and *obvious* instead of the more common distinctions of *material* and *spiritual* need, is necessary. Missionaries in modern affluent societies discover that the elaborate disguising activities of most of the population are extremely effective. The individualism and competition that define modern society makes active disguising of all types of need imperative. The image of success must be maintained at all costs.

The inadequacy of the common material/spiritual distinctions when referring to different types of human need is readily apparent. For example, the difference between the high-level executive who is an alcoholic and the skid row bum may be seen as a difference in disguise. Both may be needy in similar ways. But their positions in society and their diagnoses of needs are likely to be extremely different. In modern societies the options of effective disguises and the ability to use them make necessary a redefinition of the needy categories in terms of disguise or lack of it.

The obviously needy

The first type of target group, the *obviously* needy, is the minority in every affluent society. The obviously needy, because of the nature of their needs, live on the fringes of the mainstream of society. This minority are those who cannot, or did not choose to, succeed—at least not according to the standards of the majority of the affluent society in which they live.

What creates this obviously needy minority is often difficult to distinguish from the symptoms. "Why are there some people here living in poverty?" the missionary may ask economically comfortable neighbors. The answers may be simple: "They're too lazy, stupid, or antisocial." Or more analytical: "It is the availability of drugs. It is the breakdown of the family. It is the inequalities of our welfare system." In any case, members of the needy minority are generally viewed negatively by the mainstream majority of society.[17]

This group seems a logical target group for the missionary. She has searched for and found the neediest in this good society and hopes her message will be seen as good news, at least to this group. But something quickly becomes clear, despite the missionary's good intentions of identifying with the poor and oppressed. It turns out that modern affluent societies are organized to deal with these obvious needs, or at least the symptoms, more effectively than can the missionary. Society's vast specialized institutions carry the responsibility for providing assistance to the obviously needy.

With much of the nation having turned against social service spending, this may currently seem less true in the United States than it once was. But it is still very much the case in most affluent societies.

The obviously needy do not themselves see the established, indigenous church, much less the North American missionary, as having primary responsibility for dealing with their "real" needs. Most in the mainstream of society would agree. "Today when someone is an invalid, poor, unemployed, orphaned or widowed," writes Bruce Wilson, "we look to the government to provide some kind of social service benefits."[18]

At best both the obviously needy and the remaining majority of people in the affluent society may see the church as contributing, in a limited way, to that which secular institutions are responsible to do. All seem to agree that the missionary may fill needs in areas for which public institutions are not expected to take responsibility—that is, to provide spiritual care for those among the obviously needy who feel they need it.

If the missionary does accept this role of "spiritual specialist," she risks being seen by the target group as offering yet another possible solution among those already available from other institutions and organizations of the "establishment." She risks being seen by the obviously needy as belonging to the upper classes, to a part of society to which they themselves do not belong.

The result is that, from the viewpoint of the obviously needy, there is a vast distance socially between themselves and the missionary.[19] "The Christian church is seen to be trapped in a middle-class, establishment culture."[20]

The missionary strategically directing the gospel to the obviously needy also risks being defined within society by the majority who are not obviously needy. The missionary, like the professional social worker in modern affluent society, is not obviously needy herself. On the contrary. She is likely to be (again like the professional social worker) an educated, motivated individual with a certain amount of resources at her disposal. As the Lausanne Committee for World Evangelism observes, "our evangelistic and service programs tend to work for, rather than with, the urban poor."[21]

By working for and not with the obviously needy in modern society, the missionary earns affirmation by the mainstream majority without challenging their false assumptions that the gospel message is irrelevant for them. The missionary is given a certain acceptance and status by the majority.

She finds this acceptance difficult to reject, for the sensitive missionary is continually seeking to fit into and be accepted by her adopted society in order to be effective. She needs a certain amount of affirmation to maintain her sense of self-esteem. The result is a social position in society on which all of society seems to agree and which the missionary is inclined to accept—she belongs socially to the mainstream majority in modern affluent society.

But this is not inevitable. A social shift in the opposite direction also may be attempted. The missionary may recognize the difficulty of relating the gospel as good news to the obviously needy minority from the higher social position of the mainstream majority. She may then reject her social position as defined by society and seek to identify herself with the obviously needy. This is an exceedingly difficult step for North American missionaries in modern societies to take. The missionary risks alienation from the mainstream majority without assurance of integration or even acceptance from the obviously needy.

Even if somehow successful at integrating with the obviously needy, this missionary is likely to discover that building a healthy church entirely from within this segment of society is another matter. This is because those who have managed to slip through all of the holes in the series of safety nets that modern society has constructed are not easily integrated into normal church life. A German church planter friend of ours, after struggling for months to lead a Bible study group whose discussions repeatedly degenerated into nonsense, commented, "It slowly occurred to me that I was the only 'normal' person in the group!"

The missionary may not feel competent and indeed often is not equipped to handle the deeper problems out of which the obvious needs grow. In her efforts to establish a church within this segment of society, the missionary may become deeply involved in rehabilitation efforts. She may become so involved that she has little time or energy to devote to the majority of people in the society. In this process, the social gap between the missionary and the mainstream majority widens.

Our experience with a *Landstreicher* (street person) in Munich was not an uncommon one for missionaries in modern affluent societies. As soon as Wolfram (not his real name) showed up in our fledgling Bible study group with his dozen plastic bags bulging with all his earthly belongings, we had a full-time job. We gave him a place to sleep in our apartment. We spent hours in "conversation" with Wolfram. These tended to be mostly one-sided due to our limited knowledge of his street-level German spoken through broken, rotting teeth. We bribed him to use our shower by offering cooked meals as a reward. We became exhausted. Wolfram left.

We do not regret having attempted to help Wolfram. We continued to relate to him over a period of five years in Munich. We saw him respond positively to the practical love the little church showed him. Although we learned much from relating to Wolfram in honest moments, we recognized that during the time Wolfram lived with us most of our energies were being absorbed by him. We had nothing left for others.

The missionary can choose to direct her efforts primarily to the target group of the obviously needy. However, she must face the fact, that after she has made sincere attempts to adapt to the obviously needy, and after she has accepted a lowered social position, she still has managed to attract only a few of the obviously needy. The missionary has had a major impact on neither the obviously needy nor the mainstream majority of society despite careful strategic thinking. Yet in the process her message, method, and social position have all been affected.

The disguised needy

The other main target group in modern affluent society is the *disguised needy*. Like the obviously needy, those in this target group recognize that they have needs and are seeking solutions that will alleviate at least the symptoms of those needs. But in contrast to the obviously needy, the needs of this target group are often hidden behind a facade of well-being and contentment.

Although the search for solutions may eventually lead the disguised needy to pursue bizarre alternatives or to exhibit startling external behavior, the needs themselves have to do with the inner, personal realm of life. They have to do with "respectable" problems such as loneliness, guilt, lack of ful-fillment, meaninglessness of life, or starvation for love.

This market, cutting as it does across all socioeconomic classes, is vast. Whole industries and movements in modern affluent society offer responses to these needs ranging from ancient alchemy to New Age. This indicates the size of the market and the price people are prepared to pay for salva-tion.

The strategic-thinking missionary will be attracted to this target group for various reasons. One is its sheer size. A second is the nature of needs that seem ready-made for the gospel. A third is the eagerness with which the disguised needy pursue salvation. The possibility of building a church among these apparently successful, goal-oriented, energetic, and organized individuals who wear cologne is also an at-tractive prospect.

The salvation the disguised needy seek in affluent society has two features that cause the missionary who focuses her efforts on this group to adjust the gospel in response. Salva-tion for the disguised needy tends to be both limited and private. It is *limited* in that it is a spare-time pursuit, as Wilson says, for "people increasingly seek their salvation in the pri-vate leisure zones."[22]

It is *private* in that it involves only the individual.

> Even amongst Christians, for whom personal identity is sup-
> posed to be a matter of personal relationships—with God,
> others and nature—there is a growing emphasis upon the cult
> of the individual, concerned to find personal salvation, but
> with little sense of responsibility to the world at large.[23]

Stuart Fowler of Australia observes that

> all this is seen as a very private matter. Like daily cold show-
> ers or drinking carrot juice it is fine for those who believe in it,
> but not something that ought to intrude into the public life of
> society. It's not for everyone. It may even be that it makes
> those who believe in it better, fitter people but it remains a
> completely private matter that has nothing to do with public
> issues as such.[24]

Effects of target-group thinking

How do these expectations distort the missionary's message? The missionary, heartened by the hunger and thirst of
the disguised needy for a limited and private salvation, is
tempted to respond with a limited and private gospel.

A significant theological shift occurs. This shift may range
from being a subtle individualization of the gospel message
to a blatant prosperity doctrine. But in any case the concept
of costly discipleship will likely be minimized. The cross and
the call for self-denial will likely be weakened. The gospel
can become the means for achieving individual ends.

Not only will the message be affected, the method of communicating the good news, the packaging, will also be
adapted to meet the expectations of the consumer. In spite
of the tremendous numbers of people with disguised needs
in affluent societies, the missionary knows there is a pletho-
ra of attractive solutions offered to meet these needs. The
gospel is then seen as merely one, slightly outdated, possi-

bility among many. The missionary may thus be tempted to repackage her product and adjust the sales technique to compete.

Stuart Fowler describes this process.

> It may be tempting to respond [by] . . . remodeling our programs and stepping up our activities, designing better and bigger evangelistic programs and searching for ways of communication more attuned to a secular age. While all this may have its place, it will mean little in terms of a genuine renewal of Christian faith in our time unless we face the fundamental issue that is muting our proclamation of the gospel to our age: the church as being taken captive by the world.[25]

What happens to the social position of the missionary in this market-based approach to sharing the good news? The missionary offers answers which meet the inner, personal needs of individuals. She does so in ways compatible with the expectations of society. She is then seen as a legitimate, constructive contributor within society.

The missionary fits into the organized, upwardly mobile, professional system of modern society and may be regarded by others as being another professional. After all, the missionary, like others in the caring professions, is concerned to help people become happier, better adjusted, successful individuals within society. She can do this without challenging the status quo. She has the position, along with those she is helping, of being a good person in a good society. Her services may even be requested. For the missionary struggling for identity and recognition, this is tremendous affirmation!

But what is the price of these shifts? Fowler summarizes,

> The result is that, in spite of having, in principle, the same world-shaking, liberating faith as the first century disciples, we twentieth century Christians are not seriously disturbing the world order of our day as those disciples disturbed the

first century world order. The world has neutralized us most effectively by containing us within a narrowly confined area of life in a pact of peaceful coexistence. The price we pay is a fundamental mutilation of the gospel.[26]

If the missionary thinks about this peaceful coexistence, she may feel somewhat uneasy—especially if she compares herself with earlier disturbers of world orders such as Jesus, the early Christians, and the Anabaptists. No one is accusing her of turning the world upside-down.

These twinges of conscience about the *faithfulness* of her witness may be offset, however, by measuring the *effectiveness* of her witness. Her success, although not the kind that can be measured by how society is being affected, *can* be measured by how many individuals are responding to her message. Even if lives are not changed as in Jesus' time, or as described in Acts, or even as during the Anabaptist movement, some people are being helped nevertheless.

The missionary, recognizing this difference, may assume that what has changed are the *times.* She may reason that comparisons to earlier eras are really not possible. Her society is so vastly different (better) than that in which Jesus, the early church, and the Anabaptists witnessed, that the gospel cannot be expected to have the same kind of effects within society.

Comparisons which the strategically oriented missionary does make between herself and those just mentioned will be selective, church-growth, statistical kinds of comparisons. Other kinds of comparisons will be avoided—such as the social impact her witness is having compared with the witness of Jesus, the early church, and the Anabaptists.

This brief description of the missionary's response to the difficult and complex task of witnessing in modern affluent societies is not intended to be a complete portrayal of what can and often does happen. It only serves to show how the process of adaptation which begins with strategic thinking shapes the missionary's message, method of witness, and social place within the modern affluent society to which she has come.

Should this shaping be avoided? Can it be? Kaldor observes,

> "When one considers that on a global scale our nation [Australia] is one of the most advanced, it seems that the bulk of . . . [Australia's] Christians are among the most wealthy people in the world. This is a far cry from the social composition of the disciples or of the early church outlined in Acts."[27]

Yes, this shaping process can and should be avoided. The integrity and effectiveness, the authenticity of our missionary endeavor, are at stake. The pattern of Jesus did not follow the strategic-thinking process as described above. The witness of the early church and the Anabaptists did not begin with these kinds of strategic considerations.

To be authentic witnesses[28] we too must begin the process of contextualization at a point other than at the level of strategic considerations. To be like Jesus in our witness, we missionaries must begin our witness in new areas of mission in the modern, affluent world. We must make conscious, primary decisions about our social position in these societies. This could be called the *incarnational* alternative to the strategic approach. In the remainder of this book, we will be examining that alternative.

CHAPTER 2

Tools for Incarnational Mission

We have examined the effects of strategic thinking as the starting point for witness in modern affluent societies. We have seen how such thinking eventually affects the message, method, and social position of the missionary—and that all three of these are interwoven.

We have seen how the strategic approach, while more or less effective in reaching either obviously needy or disguised needy individuals, tends in the end to limit the missionary and the emerging church. It relegates them to positions of relative ineffectiveness in impacting society.

Jesus, the early church, and the Anabaptists witnessed from distinct positions within their societies. From these social positions, their message and method of witness was developed. These social positions of Jesus, the early church, and the Anabaptists were different from that of the church and the church's missionaries in modern affluent societies today. The social positioning is what has changed so dramatically.

Now it may be argued that while Jesus' social position was a deliberate choice in the incarnation, the social positions of the early church and the Anabaptists were due to circumstances beyond their control. As these Christians did not necessarily choose their social positions in their society, neither should we be too concerned about where we, as modern witnesses, fit into our societies. We should just communicate the good news wherever we happen to be in society.

Even if we assume that the social positions of the early Christians and Anabaptists were not due to deliberate choice, it remains true that their social positions were a primary aspect of their witness. Our social positions just happen to be consistently different from the social positions of Jesus, the early church, and the Anabaptists.

But missionaries do make choices that determine their social location without being aware of it. Because this is often done without awareness makes it no less a choice. The freedom to make alternate and deliberate choices about our social positions is an option the early church and the Anabaptists did not have. The *choice* of social location of missionaries in modern affluent societies is thus the crucial issue.

We will call the deliberate choice of social position out of which to do witness the *incarnational approach*. We will examine this feature of Jesus' ministry and the Anabaptist movement in some detail later. But first it may be helpful to explore tools that enable comparisons between the societies of Jesus, the early church, and the Anabaptists, and our own modern affluent ones.

If we can compare these societies, we will be able to compare our own social position in our societies to that of Jesus in his. If comparisons can be made, it will also be possible to find principles from those earlier models to apply to our own mission endeavors.[1]

Background for the Incarnational Approach

How missionaries perceive social groupings and their receptivity to the gospel is currently seen as crucial to communicating the gospel to those who are most receptive. Jesus told his disciples, "Open your eyes and look at the fields! They are ripe for harvest."[2] Donald McGavran urges missionaries to develop "church growth eyes" to "train [themselves] to see the many different varieties of growth and the many factors which play a significant part in each."[3] Are Jesus and McGavran urging missionaries to do exactly the same thing?

It may be true that what McGavran is calling for does carry out Jesus' intent for his disciples to some extent. But it is unlikely Jesus expected his disciples to think in the same categories as those used by modern missiologists and missionaries. The modern scientific method has given rise to completely different ways for missionaries to understand their social contexts. McGavran writes,

> More than any previous century, ours is conscious of 'the masses'. . . . That mankind should be divided into beneficiaries and victims of the social order no longer seems right to thoughtful men. . . . [This is a] radically new element in human thinking.[4]

Modern sociology determines the various social groupings within society. It does so, not by measuring receptivity to the gospel, but by measuring such other factors as income, education, or kinds of employment. Missiological analysis of a given society's receptivity to the gospel is measured in terms of these existing categories defined by social scientists. The categories themselves seem to be appropriate and helpful tools for strategic purposes.

Missiologist Eugene Nida has developed a pear-shaped diagram of social order. It divides society into classes ranging from lower-lower to upper-upper. It is used by McGav-ran to make a number of missiological points. He assumes that these socioeconomic categories are not only an ade-quate starting point for determining receptivity and devel-oping appropriate mission strategy—but an essential under-standing as well. He writes, "Until sharp definition has been made of each segment of a given society, precise thinking about it is impossible."[5]

Yet it is doubtful that viewing society as an aggregate of social groupings, ranked according to socioeconomic crite-ria, is very helpful or even realistic for missionaries in mod-ern affluent societies. Robert Ramseyer points out that

> church growth expectations vis-à-vis anthropology and the social sciences in general are unrealistic. . . . Church growth theory assumes that through proper use and development of the social sciences it will some day be possible to define the relevant data and that when the data are known it will be pos-sible in a given situation to work out the proper formulae for the steps to be taken in that field for the achievement of maxi-mum church growth.[6]

Let's examine some of these shortcomings. In modern afflu-ent societies, economic status increasingly determines social status. Alan Bond is a local millionaire folk hero from Perth, Western Australia, who gained fame in America's Cup yacht racing. He was a school dropout. Yet as a wealthy business-man, he associated with the prime minister of Australia. The financially successful son of poor immigrants in the United States can become a presidential candidate. The opportuni-ties, both legal and illegal, for dramatic economic upward mobility, independent of initial social status, are available. The opposite is true as well. A stock market crash can make paupers of millionaires overnight.

Economic categories are more open, fluid, and less deter-mined by social status in modern affluent societies than in previous times. Thus they are probably not as helpful as is often assumed for establishing receptivity to the gospel in such societies.

Receptivity has to do with attitudes and values. In affluent societies it seems that the attitudes and values of individuals are neither static nor predetermined by status. The poor may be as oriented toward upward mobility as the financially successful. The financially successful may be as disillusioned and desperate as the person on welfare, even if not obviously so. Mass media, available equally to everyone, regardless of social or economic levels, influences values independent of status.

Thus the confident assertions, based on hard statistical evidence in developing countries, that the poor are the most receptive to the gospel are often disproved in affluent societies where church membership is predominantly of the upper-middle and upper classes. It seems, then, that the traditional vertical ranking of society's classes according to socioeconomic categories poses real dilemmas for missionaries contemplating initial questions of strategy (in the strategic approach) or where to identify socially (in the incarnational approach).

Do missionaries, convinced that God identifies with the poor, reluctantly build middle- and upper-class churches to succeed in building church at all? Who are the poor in modern affluent societies? Why aren't they receptive to the gospel?

Implementing the Incarnational Approach

A model for interpreting society

The first tool needed is a framework, or model, so societies can be viewed in a way not limited to the socioeconomic categories of contemporary social sciences. The following model[7] is an attempt to provide a way of determining social groupings according to receptivity to the good news of the kingdom. The model is not meant to represent society statistically in the more common sociological categories. Rather, it is an attempt to make general observations about society in keeping with Jesus' request to his disciples to "look at the fields."

It should be stressed that the model is a theoretical one and as such should be seen as offering a missiological perspective from which to view Jesus, the early church, and the Anabaptists. This will be done by finding social categories common to the societies of Jesus, the early church, the Anabaptist movement in sixteenth-century Europe, and modern affluent ones.

As the categories used are difficult to document with objective, statistical evidence, the model is, as all social models, primarily useful in its limited, intended function. This intended function is to help explain the reception and impact of the gospel in societies in different times and places and to explore new possibilities for applications in mission today.

We will begin by attempting to determine groups of people within society according to their receptivity to the gospel and by viewing society in terms of these groupings. The criteria used to establish these groupings will be *marginality, power,* and *hope.* It seems safe to assume that the social groupings defined by these criteria are common to every organized society—including the society at the time of Jesus. This enables helpful comparisons to be made. By looking at societies in this way, it may be possible to understand where change—receptivity to the gospel and conversion—is most likely to occur at both the individual level and in society as a whole.

Marginality

The first concept is *marginality*. Marginality, as is used here, has to do with the social minority in every organized society that is not part of the majority. It refers to the minority of people not integrated into the mainstream of society. This marginalization can occur for various reasons but is not necessarily determined by economic status alone.

In some societies, for instance, most of the people who are socially integrated are relatively poor and may be exploited by the wealthy elite. In modern affluent societies, some of the marginalized may be wealthy and exploit others, the locally successful drug dealers being one example. In any case, the marginalized are a minority at one extreme end of the social spectrum.

On the opposite end of the same social spectrum is the elite, establishment minority. Its members represent institutional and social power within society.

Between the marginalized minority on one end of the spectrum and the establishment minority on the other end is the majority. The majority, although not directly involved at the top levels of power and prestige, nevertheless can participate in and benefit from establishment achievements.

The following curve illustrates the possible relative distribution of the social groupings within modern, affluent society.

Profile of Society

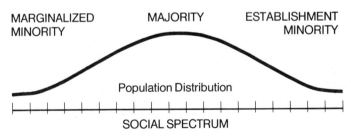

The general characteristics of the social relationships within each grouping and between the groupings within so-

ciety can also be described. For the marginalized, isolation is
the key feature. This isolation is from the rest of society in
general. But it is often marked by isolation within the group
as well, with individuals being isolated from each other. A
kind of group solidarity is sometimes evident, for instance in
neighborhood gang activities.

The social relationships of the majority can be characterized as social networks, both organic and organized. Organic relationships of the majority may be friends, family, and
neighbors. Organized relationships may include school,
church, work or business colleagues, and other voluntary
relationships.

The establishment's relationships differ from the those of
the majority in the degree of organization and power inherent in these relationships. They tend to be more highly organized and institutionally defined. Establishment relationships often take the shape of social blocks of power and solidarity.

The following diagram illustrates these three basic social
categories in society and shows how these groupings relate
to each other within the categories and to the rest of society.

Marginalization

MARGINALIZED	MAJORITY	ESTABLISHMENT
• Marginalized from both the establishment and the majority.	• Integrated socially into the mainstream.	• Represents institutional and social elite of society.
• Social isolation.	• Marginalized only from the top levels of society.	• Social block.
• Individual/gang.	• Social network.	• Highly organized.
	• Organic/organized.	• Institutional.

SOCIAL SPECTRUM

Power

The second factor, closely related to marginalization, is *power*. It is not a simple matter of power versus powerlessness in modern affluent society, for almost everyone in these societies possesses and exercises some kind of power. The difference across the social spectrum lies in the nature of the power.

The persons in the social grouping at the marginalized end of the spectrum are characterized by lack of power to change either self or circumstances for the better. The kind of power exercised tends to be survival power that can take negative, antisocial, and destructive forms. It can be chaotic and unpredictable and may elicit fear in others.

The power of the marginalized is the limited power of individuals and groups of individuals who do not have access to either the power options of the majority or the establishment. The result is that any power the marginalized may independently demonstrate is likely to be viewed from the establishment end of the spectrum as dangerous and illegitimate.

"Legitimate" power is concentrated on the other end of the social spectrum. From the establishment end, institutional power of all kinds is exercised. This power is organized and institutional in nature. It involves the control of vast resources in the economic, political, communications, legal, police, military, and educational spheres.

This form of power is both stable and predictable. Such power elicits fear and resentment in those victimized by it. Establishment power can be used to ostracize and punish those who defy it. Those who threaten to change the status quo can find themselves becoming marginalized in terms of power. Those who reap its benefits by aligning themselves with establishment power tend to grow in loyalty to it. In a democracy these institutions of power are subject to reform but the institutions themselves are jealously protected by every means at the disposal of those who are in power and benefit the most from it.

Between the two ends of the social spectrum is the majority. Certain kinds of power are potentially shared by everyone within this largest social grouping. Groups of people in the majority are able to organize themselves and participate in existing local organizations. They may vote in local and national elections and feel they are being represented. Most are employed and can choose how to spend their incomes. Their social networks potentially give them a certain amount of collective social influence.

It would seem that there are, within the majority, two basic options of power. These two basic power options arise out of two different kinds of motivations and expectations, two different kinds of values, within the majority. To put it another way, these two basic options originate and appeal to the majority from the opposite ends of the spectrum. Individuals of the majority are free to choose their response.

One option is for individuals in the majority to align themselves with, and participate in, some levels of institutional power of the establishment in hopes of maintaining or preserving the status quo. Thus calls for tougher anticrime laws, including the death penalty, can be broadly supported. Vehemently opposed, on the other hand, are increased taxes to fund programs to alleviate social inequalities which contribute to criminal behavior.

This is not necessarily a consciously selfish choice. Many believe that the status quo, although not perfect, is successfully achieving the best for the most people in society as well as in the rest of the world. The popularity in years past of "Reaganomics," with the concept of the "trickle down effect" of wealth, is one example.

Alignment with the establishment is by far the most popular choice for the majority, especially in times of prosperity and stability. This is because the apparent rightness of the assumptions of the status quo is proven in immediate personal benefits and the conviction that life conditions are improving or soon will.

Economic status does not entirely decide the attitude of the majority for, as noted earlier, even the economically poor can be upwardly mobile in their attitudes and can support the goals of the establishment. A dramatic case in point is the immense popular support of Operation Desert Storm. There 30 percent of the U.S. soldiers on the front lines were African-American, some of whose members represented economically disadvantaged groups. Yet the interviews broadcast from the front lines invariably demonstrated that these soldiers saw themselves as defending values identical to the political establishment which decided to send them there. Those likely to benefit least from the war took the highest risks to preserve the status quo by fighting the war.

Besides the power option for the majority that arises from the establishment end of the social spectrum, there is another kind of power option that originates from the marginalized end of the spectrum. There is, in modern affluent societies, a general awareness that all is not right with the world or even within good societies. The obvious inadequacies and injustices of the status quo in regard to the marginalized within modern affluent societies are obvious to all except the willfully ignorant. The oppression, hunger, and war under which much of humanity in other parts of the world suffer is well publicized in affluent societies. The other basic power option originates then because of the *inadequacies* of the status quo.

The power of the disenchanted often is expressed in the form of ideas, visions, and dreams of change—change that will produce a better, more just and humane society. These ideas, visions, and dreams can catch the imagination of some of the majority and become popularized, forming the basis for people movements.

Such visions can inspire calls for radical change, revolution, and, in extreme cases, use of violence. Martin Luther King's "I Have a Dream" speech is just one example of the power of ideas and dreams to mobilize, not only victims of injustices, but also many other individuals, especially from within the majority category.

The chart below illustrates the basic power options in society and how these relate to the marginalization categories outlined earlier.

Power

MARGINALIZED	MAJORITY		ESTABLISHMENT
	Two Basic Possibilities		
	A	**B**	
• Powerless for improvement or destructive, negative power. • Not seen as legitimate.	Power of ideas shared with others. People power. Violence sometimes a tempting option.	Power through alignment with the establishment.	• Institutional and social power. Uses the power at disposal. • Seen as legitimate.

├─┼─┼─┼─┼─┼─┼─┼─┼─┼─┼─┼─┼─┼─┼─┼─┼─┤

SOCIAL SPECTRUM

Hope

The last criterion, *hope*, is directly related to both marginalization and power. On the marginalized end of the spectrum are those without motivational hope. This social grouping represents a minority in society. Its individual members may express their hopelessness through some kind of destructive behavior toward themselves, others, or both. The surging, destructive anger, those eerie scenes of senseless looting captured by television crews during social disturbances that periodically wrack our cities, is the visible vacuum left by hope that has died.

Just as with marginalization and power, hope is not determined by socioeconomic status alone. A deprived youth from the slums becomes, against all odds, a professional basketball player. Contrast this with the youth from an upper-class suburb surrounded by every material and social advantage who commits suicide. This underscores the point that socioeconomic status is not everything. In the marginalized minority at the extreme end of the social spectrum, focused hope can potentially be raised from outside of this category.

On the opposite end of the spectrum are those whose hope lies in the preservation or improvement of the status quo. The top levels of power of the social institutions within organized society are reached only by a small minority of society. This minority can be a very loyal and committed group, for the rewards of power and prestige, being hard won, are not readily sacrificed.

Those who have reached the top rungs of the ladders of power are, in Darwinian terms, the "fittest" ladder climbers competitive society can produce. The skills learned in climbing equip them to survive at the top. Hope in this category therefore tends to be conservative, pragmatically concerned with both institutional preservation and protection of one's personal position within the institution.

For the majority between the extremes, hope is alive, at least potentially, and has two basic options. From the side of the establishment comes the enticement of the status quo and the possibility of progress for society in general and personal happiness in particular. The values of the establishment, with their conservative and self-preserving bias, seem obviously correct to many of the majority. This is especially the case when such powerful symbols as the cross or the flag are appealed to. Hope for many in the majority is essentially establishment hope of working within the status quo.

The other basic hope option originates from the marginalized end of the social spectrum. It is there that human needs are most obvious and deficiencies of the status quo most evident. Hope takes the form of visions for the possibility of a more just, humane, and peaceful world.

Such hope often results in people calling for fundamental social change. People movements of all kinds, including violent revolution, rise out of people in the majority category motivated by hope of change to the extent that they take personal risks to achieve and participate in a new social reality. This hope of the majority can potentially arouse the attention and even raise the hopes of the marginalized. Sharing of hope can result in a solidarity of some of the marginalized with many of the majority. It can eventually impact all society.[8]

It should be noted that the majority can freely choose between the two basic hope options or even to hold both simultaneously albeit inconsistently. It is possible to have deep feelings of compassion for the victims of war, for instance, while vehemently defending participation in the military.

In all modern societies the majority is constantly faced, through the media, with two strong messages: First, the reality of injustice and suffering. Second, the possibility of the "good life." The evening news, interspersed with commercial advertisements, gives both messages simultaneously.

The following chart shows the social spectrum in terms of hope and the relationship to power.

Hope

MARGINALIZED	MAJORITY	ESTABLISHMENT
	Two Basic Possibilities	
	A	**B**	

MARGINALIZED	A	B	ESTABLISHMENT
• Minimal, survival hope, without motivational dreams. • Hope can potentially be raised by either the establishment's enticements or the visionary hope of those who call for change.	Are concerned by the plight of the marginalized and lack of justice. Hope lies in the possibility for change. Are willing to take personal risks to achieve these ideals.	Are influenced by then apparent rightness of the values of the establishment. Hope lies in the preservation of the status quo.	• Hope lies in the preservation of the status quo. Attempts to propagate these values in order to win the support of the majority in the interests of self-preservation.

├─┼─┼─┼─┼─┼─┼─┼─┼─┼─┼─┼─┼─┼─┼─┼─┼─┤

SOCIAL SPECTRUM

Several summary observations need to be made. First, as pointed out earlier, the position on the social spectrum is not established solely by socioeconomic status. This *is* a factor. But in reality, especially in modern affluent societies, freedom of choice in the area of values, combined with access to information, permit movement horizontally on the spectrum in either direction.

Second, society can be seen as being on a continuum. It is not comprised of a series of sharply divided socioeconomic categories.

Third, major shifts in attitudes and values concerning hope and power within the majority occur rather easily between A and B depending on the social climate. This can occur without necessarily breaking the organic and organizational relationships within the majority category. The extreme ends of the spectrum can be seen as much more static. Real change in values and attitudes jeopardizes the position on the social spectrum, especially on the establishment end.

Finally, the minorities on the opposite ends of the spectrum have the least in common. They therefore have the least impact on one another in terms of substantial social change. The majority is, on the one hand, located socially next to both the marginalized and the establishment minorities. It thus has the potential of impacting both.

Several additional observations, when placed against the backdrop of this understanding of society, will help us understand Jarrel Pickett's statement, "God uses social forces to bring men [and women] under the influence of the gospel."[9]

What role do human aspirations, visionary longings, and dreams of utopia play in receptivity to the gospel? It seems many of these could be classified as being expressions of a basic God-given "hunger and thirst for righteousness," a longing for justice, peace, and goodness—in short, a longing for the kingdom. These longings for the kingdom, although not necessarily identified as such, are fostered whenever injustice and evil cause human oppression and suffering. In times when the social conditions are ripe, they result in people movements.

It seems that authentic Christian movements, beginning with the early church, taking place throughout history, and including the Anabaptist movement, occur when the spirit of God intersects with aspirations of people, the human longings for the kingdom. These movements could be called "people movements of the Spirit" rather than either "people movements" or "spiritual movements."[10]

Several hypotheses can now be made based on these observations.

- Jesus incarnated and preached the good news of the kingdom from social position A within the social spectrum. His message sounded appealing to those in social position A, for their hope lay in the possibility of immediate change. From this social position, Jesus exposed the fallacy of establishment hope. At the same time, he refused the use of coercive power and violence. Jesus raised the hope of the marginalized from a position of proximity to them.

- Although individuals were attracted from both ends of the spectrum, the church emerged from within the majority, primarily from social position A. It grew among those who hoped for immediate change, who were ready to take personal risks in order to achieve this.

These people were at once concerned about their own, and others' lots in life and were motivated by popular social and religious ideas. Jesus' preaching of the kingdom corresponded to their dreams of change.

They were integrated socially. The church, as it gained momentum as a people movement of the Spirit, increasingly challenged the establishment prophetically. It attracted the marginalized by visibly demonstrating the kingdom life and the power of Jesus' way. This was an authentic witness, for the good news of the kingdom was preached in the manner of Jesus, from the same social position.

- The Anabaptist movement, as with other people movements of the Spirit before and after, began in much the same way. The preaching of the kingdom coincided with the human longing for the kingdom in all its forms. The movement emerged among those whose hope lay in change, who were willing to take risks in order to participate in it. Again the witness was from the same social position as of Jesus.

In the next chapters we will test these hypotheses, beginning with the example of Jesus' witness.

CHAPTER 3

Jesus: Model of the Incarnational Approach

> Born in a stable of humble parents and a refugee in early childhood, Jesus grew up in the despised town of Nazareth. In middle life he abandoned his craft to begin the messianic mission of good news about the inbreaking of God's kingly reign, journeying throughout Palestine, often with no place to sleep. After a brief ministry, he was put to death by the power elite of the day, crucified among criminals.[1]

This brief description of Jesus suggests something of the social position from which he began his ministry. It is difficult to assume that Jesus' social position was incidental in the incarnation, a case of "blooming where one is planted." The nature of Jesus' ministry was clearly marked. He did not identify with humankind in general but deliberately identified with a distinct social grouping within society.

Jesus' social position was a primary factor in how people perceived his ministry and the impact of his words. From the beginning the good news of the kingdom appealed immediately to some and sounded ominously threatening to others. This is evident on the very first recorded occasion of Jesus' public ministry.

> The Spirit of the Lord is on me,
> because he has anointed me
> to preach good news to the poor.
> He has sent me to proclaim freedom for the prisoners
> and recovery of sight for the blind,
> to release the oppressed,
> to proclaim the year of the Lord's favor. (Luke 4:18-19)

With these powerful words, Jesus opened his public ministry. Their impact was immediate. They moved people in opposite directions. "All spoke well of him and were amazed at the gracious words that came from his lips" (Luke 4:22). But as Jesus elaborated further, the mood changed: "All the people in the synagogue were furious when they heard this" (Luke 4:28).

The reaction of people in that Nazareth synagogue listening to Jesus' inaugural address was an indication of two possible extreme responses that would sweep back and forth through society until the final tidal wave of officially sanctioned social reaction ended Jesus' life. No part of society, it seemed, could remain indifferent or apathetic to the good news of the kingdom spoken by Jesus in Palestine.

Within the society of Palestine, a predictable, general pattern of response to—and reaction against—the message and life of Jesus emerges in the Gospel accounts. With few exceptions, response to Jesus seems to have been directly related to the social position of Jesus relative to the social position of those encountering him.

Social Categories in Jesus' Society

Let us examine Jesus' society more closely. Two main broad social categories, which can be seen as two sets of contrasting pairs, are used in the New Testament to describe society: the rich and the poor; the sinners and the righteous. In addition to these broad social groupings, the main religious and political Jewish parties are also named. How did Jesus and the Gospel writers use these terms? How did they portray Jesus in relation to the social groupings to which these terms refer? Where did Jesus fit in?

The poor and the rich

We will begin by looking at the poor and the rich. The poor is one of the most important social categories used in both the Old and the New Testaments. A brief clarification by the Lausanne Committee for World Evangelism is helpful here.

> The New Testament uses a number of terms to describe the poor: the manual worker who struggles to survive on a day-to-day basis, the destitute cowering as a beggar, the one reduced to "meekness," the one brought low. We must include those weak and exhausted by manual labor, the widows and "the common people."
>
> Throughout the Bible most references indicate that the poor are the mercilessly oppressed, the powerless, the destitute, and the downtrodden.[2]

The poor then, as used in Scripture, refers to a rather broad social category. It is not used to indicate poverty alone, but social status contrasting to the social category of the rich and powerful. The term *poor*, as a social category, is used at least seventeen times in the Gospels. Jesus invariably used the term poor to refer to a social grouping about which he was positive.

In contrast, Jesus uses the term *rich* to indicate a social grouping about which he was consistently negative. Typical of Jesus' attitude is the sharp contrast between the rich and poor in Luke's Gospel. "Blessed are you who are poor, for yours is the kingdom of God. . . . But woe to you who are rich, for you have already received your comfort" (Luke 6:20, 24).

Even more fascinating is the use of the terms *sinners* and *righteous* which refer to two contrasting social categories in Jesus' society. The term sinners, when used to indicate a social grouping, as in the phrase "publicans and sinners," is used by Jesus most often in a positive way. In contrast, Jesus uses the term righteous, when indicating a social category, consistently in a negative way![3]

The well-known contrast in Matthew 9:13 sums up Jesus' usage of the terms: "I have not come to call the righteous, but sinners." The oft repeated accusation that Jesus "ate and drank with sinners" indicates his identification with that part of society. It also shows the offense the "righteous" took at this breach of social convention.

Placing the rich and poor, the sinners and righteous, on the social spectrum introduced in the previous chapter may help in visualizing Jesus' social identity and understanding the significance this had in his ministry. As in the previous models, this should be seen as an attempt to interpret society in terms of receptivity to Jesus and the good news of the kingdom using the social categories of the New Testament. This is not an attempt to define New Testament society using conventional categories of the social sciences.[4]

The first contrasting pair, the poor and the rich, represents the two opposite ends of the social spectrum. The poor would have to be located toward the marginalized end of the spectrum. As a large social category, the poor would include not only the marginalized, but at least part of the majority, as the term *common people* indicates.

In the Gospel accounts, some of the poor which Jesus encountered appear to be very marginalized. These are the lepers, the crippled, the blind, and the beggars, who live in relative isolation from the rest of society. This isolation and the lack of hope of the most marginalized of the poor is dramatically evident in the man beside the Pool of Bethesda. When asked by Jesus whether he wants to get well, he points to his isolation and lack of hope by complaining, "I have no one to help me into the pool." His next comment indicates his powerlessness. "When I am trying to get in, someone else goes down ahead of me" (John 5:7).

In contrast, the rich, as a social grouping, would need to be placed on the opposite end of the social spectrum from the poor. (This is exactly where the rich of the New Testament would want it to be!) The rich are often portrayed as self-sufficient and representing the power of the establishment. A real dedication to the protecting of the status quo is clear in Jesus' encounters with the rich and the stories he told about them.[5]

This group as a whole was not receptive to the good news. Individuals found it extremely difficult to follow Jesus. "It is easier for a camel to go through the eye of a needle," Jesus finally said, "than for a rich man to enter the kingdom of God" (Matt. 19:23).

Between the two extreme ends of the social spectrum is the majority. Moving into the majority area of the social spectrum, the poor demonstrate hope, creative action, and social integration. This is shown in the story of the paralytic whose friends lowered him down through the roof in an attempt to get him to Jesus for healing (Mark 2:4).

This story also portrays the kind of hope that the poor in the majority area of the social spectrum often exhibited—a hope in dramatic change and the readiness to take personal risks in order to participate in it. The common people in this category were those whose "hunger and thirst for righteousness" drew them around Jesus, and caused the crowds to follow him with such eagerness that they forgot to take food along (Matt. 14:13-21). Their hope was that of those who have little to lose in case of failure.

The hope of the people in the majority category had two basic forms in Palestine. On one hand there was hope for change by those who were oppressed and by those who heard their cry. On the other hand was the hope of the status quo promoted by the establishment.

The people in the majority category in Palestine seem to have been free to choose where to place their hope. They could join a people movement organized around a charismatic, antiestablishment teacher. Or they could support an anti-Roman terrorist group like the Zealots, which hoped for fundamental change.

On the other hand, they could align themselves with the establishment in hopes of personal gain or social reform. Those in the majority seem to have been able to move rather easily and quickly between options A and B on the social spectrum. The example of Judas, or the crowds at the trial of Jesus, illustrate clearly the options for people in the majority category to go either one direction or the other depending on the circumstances.

The sinners and the righteous

The second contrasting pair, the sinners and the righteous, can like the rich and the poor, be placed on the two opposite ends of the social spectrum. The social marginalization of the "publicans and sinners" is evident in the shock so often expressed on the occasions when Jesus ate with them. It seems that the sinner category paralleled, in the public opinion, the social category of the poor. The terms were at times even used interchangeably.

The story of the man born blind illustrates this popular association between poverty and misfortune with sin. "Who sinned," Jesus' disciples asked, "this man or his parents, that he was born blind?" (John 9:2) The sinners, like the poor, hungered and thirsted for righteousness, for often the sinners were the victims of social discrimination and injustice at the hands of the righteous (John 9:34).

On the other end of the spectrum from the sinners, the righteous dominated the institutional religious life. The story of the publican and the Pharisee who went into the temple to pray contrasts the two groups and depicts the attitude the righteous had toward themselves and others. They "were confident of their own righteousness and looked down on everybody else" (Luke 18:9).

Like the rich, it seems to have been almost impossible for the righteous to enter the kingdom of heaven, for they felt constantly threatened by Jesus and reacted strongly against him. Their attitude was consistently negative. At the trial and execution of Jesus, the righteous possessed and exercised not only the power of the religious institutions but also collaborated with the political and military power of the state.

Again, the majority between the two extremes on the social spectrum seem to have had freedom to choose. They could opt for the status quo values of the righteous being promoted from the establishment end. Or they could choose the values of those who cried out for change, who hungered and thirsted for righteousness from the opposite end of the spectrum. The crowds present at Jesus' trial demonstrate these two options.

The following social spectrum incorporates the social categories of poor/rich, and sinners/righteous in the social spectrum introduced earlier.

Social Categories in Jesus' Society

MARGINALIZED	MAJORITY		ESTABLISHMENT
POOR	(common people, the people, the crowds)		RICH
Man at the Bethesda Pool	Crowds who followed Jesus	Crowds at Jesus' trial	Rich young ruler
SINNERS			RIGHTEOUS

SOCIAL SPECTRUM

Social Location of Jewish Religious Parties

Where did the Jewish religious parties fit into Jesus' society? It is helpful to examine their social positions in the social spectrum to better understand their relationships and patterns of response to Jesus. The following represents an attempt to generalize about the relative social location of the significant Jewish political/religious parties mentioned in Scripture and history—the Herodians, Sadducees, Pharisees, and Zealots.

Little is known about the Herodians from the Gospels other than that they were united in their opposition to Jesus. They probably represented a political/religious party aligned with Herod the Great. That they were socially on the establishment end of the social spectrum is beyond doubt.

The Sadducees were the aristocratic conservatives of the Jewish political/religious institutions. They enjoyed the fruits of peaceful coexistence with foreign occupiers and were wary of any social change that might have threatened their favored position. They held power and were ready to use it pragmatically for the good of the nation as they understood it—stability, peace, and the preservation of the Jewish religious status quo. This category was likely limited to the elite of the religious structure.

The Pharisees, by most estimates, were a relatively small group, a minority movement within the Jewish religious system. But they seem to have held tremendous influence among the people through their aggressive devotion to the law. They sought to defend the religious status quo and seemed prepared to cooperate politically with others when this was threatened.

Although in some ways the Pharisees were a renewal movement, it was a return to an idealized past that they were championing. This seems to have made them natural allies with those who were dedicated to defending the status quo. Anthony Saldarini comments on the Pharisees,

They seek influence and resultant control among the people as religious experts. . . . Because in antiquity political authority is thoroughly enmeshed with religious teaching, practice and authority, they enter into political alliances with Herodians and are associated with Scribes who do have some political control. They are members of the retainer class, involved in community guidance and leadership, even if not in an official capacity. They have community standing according to the prevailing system of prestige and honor, and they probably function as patrons and brokers for the people, even if they have lost direct political power.[6]

Although there seems to be no real consensus among scholars on the social location of the Pharisees, their use of power, the nature of their hope and their disdain for the sinners makes it clear that they belonged toward the establishment end of the social spectrum.

The Zealots, although not mentioned in the Gospels, are the subject of much interesting speculation. This underground political/religious terrorist group was motivated by revolutionary visions and prepared to use violence to overthrow the Roman occupying force and the infidel establishment with which it collaborated. Although the Zealots took the side of the poor and the oppressed, they avoided contact with publicans and Romans.

We can now include the main Jewish parties on the social spectrum in order to visualize their social position within society and their relative position to that of Jesus.

Jesus and the Jewish Parties in Society

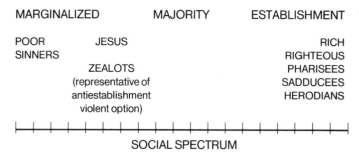

MARGINALIZED	MAJORITY	ESTABLISHMENT
POOR	JESUS	RICH
SINNERS		RIGHTEOUS
	ZEALOTS	PHARISEES
	(representative of	SADDUCEES
	antiestablishment	HERODIANS
	violent option)	

SOCIAL SPECTRUM

Our hypothesis about Jesus' social position is this: Jesus incarnated and preached the good news of the kingdom from social position A (part of the majority but listening to the marginalized) rather than B (part of the majority but listening to the establishment).

Effects of Jesus' Social Position on His Reception

What effects did the social position of Jesus have on the way his message was received? Jesus, in social position A, raised the hope of the marginalized from a position of proximity to them. His message sounded appealing to those in social position A, for their hope lay in the possibility of immediate change. From this social position, the establishment hope was exposed as false. The establishment reacted by trying desperately to discredit Jesus.

The marginalized welcome Jesus

Viewed in this way it is clear why the social location of Jesus was a fundamental choice in the incarnation. Jesus' social position next to the marginalized poor and sinners enabled him to share the good news of the kingdom in a way that raised their hopes. As an integrated person, he could communicate the good news in terms the marginalized immediately recognized as good. As hope was raised among hopeless individuals, these persons move socially toward Jesus. This move was toward both radical change and social integration.

Who appreciated Jesus and listened with eager interest to his teachings? The crowds around position A, those who hungered and thirsted for righteousness, those looking for change and willing to take personal risks to participate in it. These were the blessed.

Jesus was one of them. His teaching corresponded with their yearnings for the kingdom. Jesus' message fed their hopes for immediate change as well as their disillusionment with the establishment in bringing about substantial, immediate change. The disciples were also likely from this social location. The beginnings of a people movement of the Spirit, realized at Pentecost, occurred among the majority in position A.

The establishment rejects Jesus

The establishment inevitably heard Jesus' message in terms of their own and Jesus' social position. They recognized that Jesus was ministering from a social position similar to the Zealots. Identifying Jesus in any way with the Zealots is a disquieting exercise. But it is easy to understand why he was viewed, from the social distance of the establishment, as a Zealot. John Howard Yoder writes that Jesus

> was perceived by some of His followers, and by the Herodians and Sadducees, as the nearest thing to a Zealot, and executed by the Romans on the grounds that he was one. He used their language, took sides with the poor as they did, condemned the same evils they did. . . .[7]

Individuals such as Nicodemus sought to understand Jesus' message from across the social distance that divided them. However, the establishment as a block generally reacted against a man and a message they perceived as threatening the status quo and the privileges they enjoyed. Their reaction to this threat is evident in the many encounters Jesus had with the "scribes and Pharisees." It reached its ugly climax at Jesus' trial, when the establishment persuaded the majority B that Jesus was a threat for everyone.

Jürgen Moltmann has observed that the higher classes, the establishment, were organized. In contrast, "the people" were unorganized. From the establishment's point of view, Jesus was dangerous because he focused the hopes of the people, giving rise to a disquieting form of power. "Jesus identified himself with the people and he proclaimed the gospel of the kingdom of God to these 'poor' and made present their liberation in words, parables and healings."[8]

Does this mean that the good news announced by Jesus is to be seen as nothing more than an articulation of the popular expectations of the people? Is the salvation Jesus preached to be understood only in terms of the immediate demonstrations of liberation that ignited the masses? Not at all! Jesus' message of good news did and does include personal forgiveness of sin. Yet Jesus' presentation of the gospel cannot be limited to such an understanding.

E. Stanley Jones wrote in 1935,

> . . . . [Jesus] announced his programme. He closed the book, gave it to his attendant and said: 'Today hath this Scripture been fulfilled in your ears.' In other words: 'Today, so far as I am concerned, this programme begins.' And it did."[9]

Salvation, as demonstrated and proclaimed by Jesus, was immediately relevant—but not limited to the immediate. It marked a radically new beginning of present change and future possibilities.

Thiessen puts Jesus' announcement of salvation in its sociological context: "The Jesus movement not only emerged from a social crisis but also articulated an answer to this crisis which does not have a sociological derivation."[10]

Jesus ministers to all social groupings

It should be noted also that Jesus did not identify himself with one social grouping to the exclusion of others. Jesus did not exclude the Pharisees, for instance. They excluded Jesus. Albert Nolan writes, "To love them [the poor] to the exclusion of others is to do nothing more than indulge in another group solidarity. Jesus did not do this."[11]

It also should be clear that Jesus completely rejected the Zealots' use of violence to bring about change. The Zealots, the crowds, and even the disciples misunderstood the nature of the kingdom Jesus proclaimed and the way it was to be realized.

It is not these misunderstandings however, that explain the attraction of Jesus' message. Jesus was popular among the poor and the change activists because they perceived the good news to be genuinely good for *them*. This they understood, at least partially, because of Jesus' social location.

A marginalized/majority coalition becomes the church

Thus the church, beginning with the disciples, formed around Jesus in the same social location in which Jesus had lived and proclaimed the good news. Although individuals were attracted from both extreme ends of the social spectrum, the church emerged from within the majority social grouping, primarily around position A. These people were at once concerned about their own and others' lot in life *and* motivated by popular social and religious ideals. Jesus' preaching of the kingdom matched their dreams.

This genuine people movement of the Spirit, known as the early church, gained momentum in the societies it entered. As it did so, it increasingly challenged the establishment prophetically. Simultaneously it attracted the marginalized by visibly demonstrating the kingdom life and the power of Jesus' way. Jesus and the early church can be depicted in their society in the following way:

Jesus and the Early Church in Society

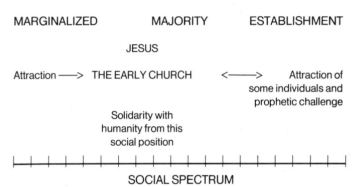

Does Jesus' social location in the incarnation have missiological implications for other societies in other times and places? In the next chapter, we will examine whether or not the Anabaptist movement began in the same social location as Jesus and the early church—and whether it impacted society in similar ways.

CHAPTER 4

Anabaptism: A People Movement of the Spirit

"The people were running after them as though they were living saints," lamented a frustrated Swiss Protestant Reformer Heinrich Bullinger of Zurich in 1531 about the Anabaptists.[1]

So it must have appeared to the members of that society's establishment. Their positions of privilege and power in both church and state structures were being threatened. A movement that seemed to capture the hopes and dreams of the common people during the ten years following the Peasants' War was swiftly spreading.

How could this left wing of the Protestant Reformation have succeeded in being seen by the establishment as a threat? So dangerous was the movement considered that its leaders and members were savagely persecuted and eventually driven to death and exile by its enemies.

The adherents of this voluntary Christian movement confessed themselves strangers and pilgrims on earth. Their leaders glorified suffering and martyrdom and called for a complete separation of church and state. A heightened sense of eschatology provided inspiration. How could such precepts have been so attractive to the common people?

"These people [the Anabaptists] were at the right time in the right place, employing the right methods," Hans Kasdorf maintains.[2] This is obviously true. But what does "right" mean when speaking of time, place, and methods? Is this to be understood as a productive coincidence of history and geography in which the Anabaptists found themselves and out of which they developed an effective mission strategy? If this were the case, the Anabaptist movement would have very limited missiological meaning for missionaries today. I believe, however, that the "right place" was more than a matter of coincidence.

The simultaneous rejection and popularity of the Anabaptists by different groups of people in sixteenth-century Europe bears striking resemblance to the socially determined responses to Jesus in his society. Like Jesus, the early Anabaptist leaders proclaimed the good news of the kingdom at all times. They proclaimed the kingdom in bad times, times of repression and rebellion, times of violence and counterviolence, times of surging human hope and crushing despair. The Anabaptists, as did Jesus, attracted enthusiastic interest among the common people. The Anabaptists, like Jesus, attracted the attention of the establishment as well, along with its alarm and eventually its fury.

The Anabaptists' Social Location

Might the Anabaptists, like Jesus, have been in the right place *socially* for their time? Were their methods, which attracted the attention of significant numbers of people and eventually affected all society, right precisely because of this right *social location*? By looking at the Anabaptist movement with these questions, we may find missiological principles in the Anabaptist movement applicable in modern affluent societies.

Earlier I stated that the Anabaptist movement, like other people movements of the Spirit, began where the preaching of the kingdom coincided with the popular longing for the kingdom in all its forms. This was especially the case among those whose hope lay in change, among people willing to take personal risks to participate in change. Much evidence supports this assertion.

Anabaptists and the Peasants' War

The Anabaptist movement must be seen in the context of a larger social movement—the Peasants' War. This short-lived and bloody social upheaval of 1525 involved peasants, underprivileged commoners from both rural areas and towns, manual laborers, and artisans. But it was most often *led* by nonpeasants. It is estimated that of the 300,000 participants in the revolt 100,000 were killed.[3]

Anabaptist historian James Stayer writes,

> The Peasants' War was a much broader historical phenomenon than Anabaptism . . . it spread faster than Anabaptism, reaching other parts of Switzerland, the Tyrol, Franconia, Hesse and Thuringia before Anabaptism. In these regions, after an interval of some months or years, former peasant rebels became Anabaptists, sometimes prominent Anabaptists. This permits us to examine the possibility, suggested by Marxist historians . . . that Anabaptism was to some degree a religious aftereffect of the Peasants' War.[4]

It is not necessary for our purposes to describe in detail either the repressive social practices and unfair economic conditions that led to the popular, bloody rebellion or the Peasants' War itself—other than to note that it has been called an "authentically German revolution with genuine mass support (and the only one there had ever been!)"[5] More important in answering questions about the "right place" of the Anabaptists in their society is the possibility of connections the Anabaptists had with the Peasants' War.

The work of Claus Peter Clasen attempts to minimize the possible linkages between the peasant uprising and the Anabaptism.[6] However, "most scholars active in Anabaptist studies now think that there was a significant connection between Anabaptism and the Peasants' War."[7]

But how could a peaceful, spiritual movement have been an "aftereffect of the Peasants' War"—or any war for that matter? John Driver comments,

> While sixteen-century Anabaptism was certainly a religious movement, it was also a social movement. Recent studies have shown that the religious and social views held by the peasants and the Anabaptists overlapped considerably.[8]

Driver lists seven areas in which the revolutionaries and the Anabaptists were in agreement.

- Both groups insisted the gospel was relevant to social and economic realities.
- Both protested the paying of taxes to the church.
- Both rejected structures which perpetrated class distinctions.
- Both called for human freedom.
- Both sought independence from church control.
- Both were movements of resistance to the established authorities.
- Both groups wanted nonviolent change to fuller social justice and equality (although the peasants were prepared to use force.)[9]

It is this overlap of social and religious views of restless peasants and Anabaptist missionaries which is of missiological importance. The social location which the above overlap makes evident determined how the Anabaptists were viewed by the rest of society. It helps explain their popular appeal among the masses—as well as the alarm and reaction among the authorities.

The revolutionary message and method of the Anabaptist missionaries can be best understood in this way: It was developed and proclaimed by a group of people who shared (along with many others in their society) not only many of the same *ideals* but also a *social position* within their society.

How was it that "spreading Anabaptism and the spreading Peasants' War indisputably mingled"?[10] What was the social context of this interplay and solidarity?

"The last and most dangerous time of this world has come upon us,"[11] declared the fiery Anabaptist missionary Hans Hut. So it must have seemed, not only for a radical Anabaptist evangelist with a burning apocalyptic vision, but also for the defeated revolutionaries of the Peasants' War. And for the bewildered citizens, caught between ideological fronts in the violent "Christian wars," as well as for the craftsmen, searching for enough work to feed their children. Yes, for most of the population of German-speaking Europe in 1525, Hans Hut's words made immediate sense.

The dream of a great number of the common people was for change at every level of the church-state structures which dictated so much of life. This dream of change had been awakened to the level of active hope as idealistic voices encountered widespread dissatisfaction in the centers of urban learning.[12]

For some time, the humanists had been denouncing the repression of the church-state structures of their day. They were calling for a return to a kind of primitive Christianity where freedom, dignity, and meaningful participation in society by the common people would be possible. Anti-property idealism was a popular theme among the humanists. Above all, the humanists inspired the common people with their conviction that humans had not only the capability but the *responsibility* for creating a better society.

The Reformers, in spearheading the demand for change in the church, were instrumental in transforming the common people's dissatisfaction into active hope. Here was a revolution of conscience that caught the imagination of the masses. Zwingli, Luther, and other Reformers had dared challenge the Catholic monolith. As the foundations of that supposedly unshakable institution began to crack, hope for a complete reform of society burst into open flame. The common denominator of the masses, whether revolutionary or reformist in orientation, was the desire for "das Besserung des Lebens" (improvement of life). Now was the time for change!

Sadly, the revolt of 1525 was crushed by the authorities. However, the bitter defeat of the rebels in the Peasants' War did not end either the conditions or the popular sentiments that led to the uprising. Gerhard Zschäbitz has commented,

> After the Peasants' War, revolutionary impulses continued to be lively among the masses—in changed form, to be sure, and adapted to the new situation of terrible defeat . . . [Embitterment of the masses] appears to have been fed by the war-levies and fines that followed, by the continuing persecution. . . . This resentment was also fed, no doubt, by the unqualified condemnation of the uprising by representatives of Lutheranism, from whom, at the beginning of the open struggle the peasants had expected at least moral support, totally misjudging the class ties which made such support impossible.[13]

Many in Germany were still clamoring for change. However, hope had been shattered that this would come through reform of state and church structures from which they were personally excluded. Many in the majority group were emphatically challenging the assumptions on which medieval society had been structured—the principle of authority. Clasen describes the phenomenon. "The boldness of the Anabaptists in defying authority suggests a distinct democratic tendency in sixteenth century Germany. The time was past when common people meekly submitted to orders from church or government."[14]

The Peasants' Revolt had been crushed, but in dropping the weight of authority on the masses, the church-state establishment had crushed as well the toes of their own credibility. The establishment, hopping about on damaged Catholic-Reformed feet of clay, could no longer restrict the hope and power choices of the majority.

Social Groupings During the Reformation

A look at the location of these social groupings on the social spectrum may make comparisons to Jesus and the early church possible.

In terms of marginalization, hope, and power, the population of German-speaking Europe following the Peasants' War could be seen as fitting into the three main social categories introduced earlier—the establishment, the marginalized, and the majority.

The establishment

The establishment minority group was made up of those at the top of the social, political, religious, and economic structures of their time. Those in this category would have been political rulers, the clergy, the wealthy, and at least part of the educated.

The main Protestant Reformers would have to be placed in this group. This is because they, like the Catholic church authorities whom they challenged, placed their hope in the retention of some form of *corpus christianum* ideal. Christendom, as they saw it, needed to be maintained by structures of authority and power. And these structures would be ready, when necessary, to wield the sword. Such Protestant reformers were threatened by the popular, radical change for which some in the majority were calling.

The marginalized

The marginalized minority could be placed at the other end of the social spectrum. Again, these could be seen as being those marginalized from both the establishment and the majority. They had at their disposal neither the options of establishment power nor the power options of the majority. While the marginalized were without motivational hope, their hope potentially could be raised from outside their social category by either the establishment or the majority.

The majority

The greatest portion of the population, the majority, could be seen as being located between the establishment and the marginalized. All those in this group would have experienced to varying degrees the impositions of the authority structures of church, state, or both. The majority would not have shared directly in the power of the establishment. Yet following the Reformation's challenge of the old church-state authority, new hopes had been awakened. New choices for participatory power for the majority began to emerge.

One choice for the majority was continued alignment with the power of an establishment engaged in maintaining the status quo or forcing some kind of official reform. The newer possibility for the majority was to align *against* the establishment by joining a popular movement wanting more drastic change.

Hope for the majority also had two basic options. One was an establishment hope of either retaining or reforming the status quo. This was a very enticing option—for the power and apparent rightness of the establishment was overwhelming. The ready use of the sword was also persuasive!

On the other hand, the visions and dreams of those calling for radical change, whether humanists, revolutionaries, or radical reformers, gave the majority another option for hope. Peasants, craftsmen, and educated idealists taking this option shared a common hope—a conviction that radical change was necessary to solve the problems of the existing structures of church and state. They shared the view that the establishment was in some way at fault. They saw themselves as instrumental in bringing about this change and were willing to take personal risks to participate in it. Violence was a tempting option.

Using these observations we can now illustrate the patterns of social groupings on the social spectrum.

Social Categories in the Anabaptists' Society

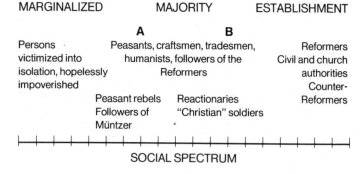

MARGINALIZED	MAJORITY	ESTABLISHMENT
	A	**B**	
Persons victimized into isolation, hopelessly impoverished	Peasants, craftsmen, tradesmen, humanists, followers of the Reformers	Reformers Civil and church authorities Counter-Reformers
	Peasant rebels Followers of Müntzer	Reactionaries "Christian" soldiers	

SOCIAL SPECTRUM

The Reformers could be seen as being more or less of the establishment, for they relied heavily on the existing power structures. Despite their rhetoric, their hope was in the retention of a reformed status quo. The Reformers' appeal initially was broad among the majority. As their establishment bias became obvious, however, segments of the majority became increasingly disillusioned.

Clustered around position A (see chapter 2) in the majority were those whose rising hope in radical change had turned to disillusionment as the intrinsic establishment bias became obvious. Clustered around position B in the majority were those whose hope continued to be in either the reform of the status quo as promoted by the Reformers or the retention of the status quo as the counter-Reformers advocated.

Anabaptist solidarity with social position A

Where did the Anabaptists fit on this social spectrum? A key event in the emergence of the Anabaptist movement occurred when several followers of Ulrich Zwingli, the Swiss Reformation leader in Zurich, rejected several of Zwingli's key social controls—infant baptism and coercive power. This rejection placed these Anabaptist leaders, from the beginning, in a conflictual position with the Reformers and their establishment bias. As the movement gained momentum, this social distance increased.

The eventual violent opposition to the Anabaptists by both the Reformation leaders and the Catholic church in German-speaking Europe firmly established the Anabaptists' social position toward the marginalized end of the spectrum. The Anabaptists were in position A in the majority category. This was also the social location of Thomas Müntzer, who led the religious armed rebellion. It was the location of the peasant rebels.

It is easy to understand why the Anabaptists, from the perspective of the establishment, were seen to be in the same camp as the peasant rebels, and why the Anabaptists were perceived to be a threat that had to be dealt with so drastically. It is equally easy to understand why the masses in the majority, disillusioned with the Reformers' halfway measures, would look to the left wing of the Reformation, the Anabaptists, with such eager interest. The Anabaptists were socially in solidarity with this part of the population.

From this social position A, the Anabaptists preached the good news of the kingdom of God. Was the message of the Anabaptists shaped by their social position? Were the Ana-

baptists participating, perhaps unwittingly, in a popular social movement? Were they preaching a gospel of revolution
as Marxist historian Gerhard Zschäbitz believed?[15] Or was
the message one of pious, noninvolved faithfulness—a message misunderstood by the revolutionaries, as others have
maintained?[16]

One Anabaptist missionary provides a fascinating model
to which we can look in answering these questions. "The al-
mighty God will punish them [the lords] and all who op-
pose the truth; they will all perish in disgrace, and it is now
the time when they will be defeated, and the peasants have
the power!"[17] These inflammatory words were spoken by
Hans Hut, a revolutionary bookseller participating in the
Peasants' Revolt.

Hut was to become "one of the greatest evangelists and
congregation founders of the whole left wing of the Reformation . . . the Apostle Paul of the south German Anabaptist
movement."[18] After joining the Anabaptists, the language of
Hut the evangelist was marked by his continuing identification with those of the majority clamoring for immediate
change.

Martin Haas notes that the Reformation in general

> moved on a broad wave of anti-clericalism. Hut's message of-
> ten reflected the sentiments of the common people. The
> priests as a class were depicted as selfish, depraved, unedu-
> cated, greedy, drunken. . . . Whoever referred to the priests
> as filthy bellies and pigs could count on widespread approv-
> al. . . . The audience pricked up its ears and missed nothing as
> soon as someone thundered against the clergy.[19]

From the position of solidarity with the sentiments of the
majority in position A, Hut spoke to an eager, appreciative
audience.

Hut's message, typical of other Anabaptist missionaries,
challenged the authority of the establishment at all levels.

"Like the revolutionaries the Anabaptists appealed to a law that ranked above positive law: in their case, to divine law."[20] In rejecting the right of the clergy to decide doctrinal questions, Hut was rejecting, as were the revolutionaries, traditional church authority.

He rejected the absolute authority of the state as well. "Like Müntzer, Hut identified the godless above all with the spiritual and secular lords,"[21] but "whereas Müntzer chose the path of violent revolution, [Hut now] only condemned the existing political institutions as unchristian."[22] This could conceivably be interpreted as being a nonpolitical message. However, it certainly was not seen that way by those in the majority clustered around social position A, who shared such convictions about their secular rulers.

Neither were Hut's views seen as nonpolitical by the establishment. From their point of view the Anabaptists' message "had dangerous implications. By condemning law courts, oaths, the legal use of force, and indeed, government itself as unchristian, the peaceful brethren became a potential threat to civilization."[23] Hut's message was seen positively by the antiestablishment majority and negatively by the church and state establishment.

In contrast to his negative and even hostile attitude toward the "evil" establishment, Hut displayed a much more positive attitude toward his former fellow-revolutionaries and many others of the majority to whom he preached his message. This attitude is summarized by Wolfgang Schaüfele.

> In the eyes of the Anabaptists, the people had been led astray and were in darkness . . . but these very "heathen" were the raw material, the building blocks of the new Christian community. . . . Hans Hut, with his perceptive view for mission possibilities, concluded that outside of the Anabaptist fellowships, there were many goodhearted people who had a desire for the truth.[24]

Hut (and other Anabaptist missionaries) preached the good news of the kingdom in ways corresponding to his social position. He shared with the peasants their negative, oppositional attitude toward the establishment. The message from this social position reinforced Hut's identity with the majority A and against the establishment, moving them to hope and fury respectively. Were these different responses due to a misunderstanding of the message?

Clasen notes, "The peasants were motivated not by an abstract religious principle, such as putting into practice the Sermon on the Mount, but by a desire for social and economic change."[25]

Zschäbitz puts it in Marxist terms.

> The ideology of the Anabaptists expresses the temper of the masses after the high point of the early bourgeois revolution. . . . Through the study of court records it becomes evident that sympathies for Anabaptist teachings were very widespread . . . we encounter plebeians and representatives of the pre-proletariat, artisans of certain crafts, peasants, but also now and again representatives of the educated classes, all struggling for a new, organizing ideology.[26]

Hut's message was both shaped by and directed to the social grouping with which he identified. One of the characteristics of Hut's message, termed by church historian Roland Bainton as a "heightened sense of eschatology,"[27] was a feature of the Anabaptist movement in general. What would a message of eschatological hope have in common with revolutionary hope? Bainton analyses the relationship between eschatology and revolution.

> Strictly speaking the two are incompatible. Eschatology believes in an imminent divine event to shatter the present scheme of history and to be inaugurated without the hand of man. Revolution depends upon human instruments. But the one idea can readily pass into the other.[28]

Hut seems to have fanned the dying embers of revolutionary hope to a flame of eschatological hope. In so doing the missionary joined hands with the revolutionaries.

It is important to note that there were profound distinctions between the Anabaptists and the revolutionaries. However, these distinctions were not questions of whether or when dramatic change should occur. The single major difference between Hut's and the other Anabaptists' message and the revolutionary ideology of the majority was this: who would initiate the kingdom—God or people?[29]

Other themes in the message of Hans Hut and fellow Anabaptist missionaries, such as inevitable judgment and temporary suffering, expressed ideas compatible to the hopes and experiences of the social grouping to which the Anabaptists belonged. It is not possible here to examine the overlap of social expectations and the Anabaptist missionaries' message in each of these areas. But the evidence is overwhelmingly consistent: the Anabaptists preached and lived after the model of Jesus. They were authentic witnesses.

John Howard Yoder has commented, "What most men *mean* by 'revolution,' the *answer* they want, is not the gospel;

The Early Anabaptist Movement in Society

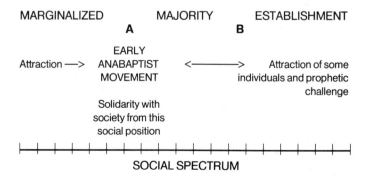

but the gospel if it be authentic must so speak as to answer the *question* of revolution. This Jesus did."[30] So did Hans Hut and other Anabaptist missionaries. The social spectrum below depicts the social location of the Anabaptists and the impact of this movement within society.

The evidence is that the Anabaptists, like Jesus, identified themselves with the social grouping within the majority who hungered and thirsted for righteousness. The Anabaptists, like Jesus, built on the hopes of this social grouping for immediate change. Their message of the kingdom went beyond their contemporaries' limited hope in the sword as an instrument of change. They called the people to an immediate "revolutionary subordination"[31] of a new human community which would live out kingdom values independent of the approval or disapproval of the establishment.

We have seen that the establishment, in the sixteenth century as in Jesus' day, perceived the good news as proclaimed from position A in the majority to be threatening, for it challenged the status quo to which they were committed.

The Anabaptist movement, like the early Christian movement, is an example of a "people movement of the Spirit," where the Spirit of God intersects with human aspirations and longings. The Anabaptist movement bore the marks of Jesus' witness—popularity, social impact, and suffering. In the next chapter we will examine and compare the mission endeavor in modern, affluent societies and begin to look for possibilities for the kind of authenticity we have been examining.

CHAPTER 5

The Church in Modern Affluent Societies

From the evidence we have seen, it seems clear that Jesus, the early church, and the early Anabaptists all began to witness from a similar distinct social position within their societies. From this position their message and method of witness was developed.

How does the social position of the church in modern affluent societies compare with that of Jesus and the early Anabaptists? How has the church's message and methods of witness in these societies been affected by their social position?

The contrasts between churches in modern affluent societies and that of Jesus, the early church, and the Anabaptist movement are conspicuous. The social location of the church in these societies tends to be far from that of Jesus in his society.

The impact of the church's witness is also vastly different. The church's general affirmation of the establishment on the one hand and the social distance between itself and the marginalized on the other stand in marked contrast to the experience of Jesus.

Social Options in Society

Let us examine the main features of modern affluent societies that are similar to the societies we have been examining. We will then compare the location of our own churches to that of Jesus.

Our own modern affluent societies are similar to the society of Jesus and the Anabaptists in that they too are like a spectrum—with the establishment on one end and the marginalized on the opposite end. The majority in these societies is somewhere between the two minorities on the extreme ends.

There are, of course, differences. Modern affluent society is far more complex. The social forces that shape the spectrum are different in many ways. In affluent societies, for instance, the truly marginalized may belong to this social grouping for different reasons than in the time of Jesus. Leprosy does not marginalize any longer but social marginalization still occurs and can be determined by new varieties of "leprosy," such as AIDS.

The highly developed social security safety nets in some societies prevent some individuals from slipping quickly, or obviously, into marginalization. On the other hand, ambitious and sometimes devious persons can break into the establishment elite with amazing speed under the right conditions.

Yet in spite of this, the basic shape of the spectrum remains. For the majority between the two extreme ends of the spectrum, the two basic options for hope are as real and convincing as ever. Due to global communication, the reality of injustice and the resulting plight of the poor is close to home, no matter where in the world it occurs. At least some flaws of the domestic economic and political systems are relentlessly publicized by the media.

The dreams of a better society are still with us, in spite of the numbing consumerism by which affluent society is marked. There are still those who hunger and thirst for righteousness. Those calling for change are as articulate as ever. Some have access to the media.

On the other hand, establishment values which saturate society are more seductive than ever. We are blanketed with the carefully crafted propaganda of the establishment, now managed by experts.

The Church's Struggle: Marginalization or Establishment?

Since the time of Jesus, the church has been tempted in two ways. One is to seek to survive by withdrawing from engagement with society. The other temptation is to seek to flourish by becoming legitimate and respectable. The seduction here is the church's alignment with the establishment at the risk of losing its authentic character.

It has always been difficult for a people movement of the Spirit to long remain socially at the position in which it began. That is because these movements result in tension, fear, and reprisals from the establishment end of the spectrum.

French sociologist of religion Henri Desroche has described the direction that messianic movements tend to take after a period of living in tension with their society.

> According to Desroche, following the impact of a messiah upon a socially, politically, and economically and religiously oppressive human context, a three-directional explosive movement tends to appear as followers believe and follow the promise of a new holistic humanity or Kingdom.[1]

Desroche's first direction points to a promised coming reality and works at its creation. This is what Jesus and the early Anabaptists were engaged in. Desroche maintains that if this messianic community encounters sustained resistance and unrelieved tension in society, two other directions are likely to be taken.

Withdrawal

One possibility is to choose the pietistic, withdrawal route and thus remain "faithful." This minimizes the movement's threat to society and consequently society leaves the movement in peace. Lesslie Newbigin laments the fact that, following the demise of *corpus christianum*—with its synthesis of public and private life—the church has accepted the division of the two as normal. "In so doing we are accepting what the New Testament church refused to accept."[2]

The deeply ingrained doctrine of two kingdoms, with its division of spiritual and temporal life, has led much of the church to separate and hold apart private faith from public life. "What God joined together in Christ is thus put asunder. And as a result both are corrupted," Jürgen Moltmann grieves.[3]

The pietistic, withdrawal route, so tempting to many evangelical churches today (including the spiritual heirs of the Anabaptists, the Mennonites), appears on the surface to be a faithful response to the wickedness of society. In fact, this option gives tacit support to the status quo in exchange for religious noninterference. The establishment is not threatened. Peaceful coexistence prevails. The religious freedoms enjoyed by the church fosters a sense of gratitude.

The long-term effect is an increasing economic and political conservatism of the church. There is a trend to form coalitions of resistance with the establishment against anything that would threaten to alter the social order of things and the church's own secure place within it.

Joining the establishment

The other option for the church, according to Desroche, is to become socially oriented, part of the legitimate, established, and orderly society. For the past 200 years, the liberal dream of progressive social reform was the basis for a high level of cooperation between mainline churches and social institutions.

This has often resulted in the church's overt sanction and defense of the status quo. Newbigin points out, as one example, that

> traditional Christian ethics had attacked covetousness as a deadly sin. The 18th century, by remarkable inversion, found covetousness not only a law of nature but the engine of progress by which the purpose of nature and nature's God was to be carried out.[4]

The rise of the "new religious right" in the United States has seemed to provide the church with an alternative to the old liberal ideals and agendas. Yet the new right actually demonstrates the same phenomenon of overt sanction and defense of the status quo by the church. The stated objectives are different, but the effect on the social position of the church in society is the same.

The church taken captive

The options of either pietistic withdrawal or establishment involvement have been, and continue to be, temptations for the church in modern affluent societies. These options determine the social position of the church. The message and method of the church's witness to the rest of society is developed and carried out from this social location.

Stuart Fowler of Melbourne, Australia, identifies the "fundamental issue that is muting our proclamation of the Gospel to our age: the church has been taken captive by the world." He describes this captivity.

> It is not a captivity by force. The heads of the Christian community are not gaoled [jailed], its members are not hounded,

its property is not confiscated. Superficially it has never been freer. Yet, like Samson shorn of his hair, while remaining a visible presence in the world the church, by and large, has lost its power to seriously challenge the world. Instead of being the prophetic community of God's kingdom in the world the church has been swallowed up in the world's secular order.

It is a captivity to which we consent willingly. The benefits and privileges and the freedom from persecution that come from a secure place as recognized and respected, even privileged, institutions of existing social order of the world makes our captivity very comfortable and inviting.

We even go beyond consent to vigorous defense of our captivity as right and proper. When any of our number threaten to disturb our peaceful co-existence with the world by fundamental criticism calling for reform of structural distortions in the existing social order we nervously hasten to distance ourselves as a community from them. We warn of the danger of confusing the gospel with social action and remind everyone that the church's mission is of personal salvation.

The tragedy is that many of us see nothing wrong with this; we do not see that it enmeshes us in a profound worldliness and that the peace, security and privilege we enjoy has been gained at the expense of a serious reduction of the world-shaking, life-encompassing biblical dynamic of the gospel to a mutilated private gospel of personal piety and morality robbed of its power to challenge the world.[5]

The Lausanne Committee for World Evangelism in its paper "Christian Witness to the Urban Poor" writes,

> The Christian church is seen to be trapped in a middle-class, establishment culture. There is an image of the church as aligned with the rich and powerful, which is confirmed by the social mobility drift of Christians from the urban poor to the middle-class areas and attitudes.[6]

Patterns of the Church in Modern Society

MARGINALIZED   MAJORITY   ESTABLISHMENT

EXAMPLES OF SOCIAL GROUPINGS

A   **B**

Drug addicts, dropouts, AIDS victims, antisocial, impoverished	Idealistic change, activists of all kinds including peace activists, environmentalists, organizers of alternative schools, feminists, etc.	Upwardly mobile, moral majority, new religious right, etc.	Representatives of church and state institutions: politicians, clergy, high level administrators

Typical Social Position of the Church

- Views establishment values as essentially Christian values
- Interested in self-preservation and legitimization
- Interested in preserving the status quo
- Makes alliances with establishment out of self-interest
- Seeks to influence establishment from within or position B
- Views change activists negatively and tends to ignore them, condemn them, or "evangelize" individuals from this group
- May seek to reach individuals from the marginalized group with "the gospel" from an establishment position

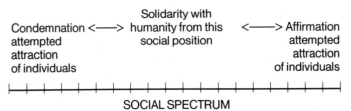

JESUS   CHURCH

Condemnation <——>   Solidarity with humanity from this social position   <——> Affirmation
attempted   attempted
attraction   attraction
of individuals   of individuals

SOCIAL SPECTRUM

We will use our now-familiar social spectrum to plot the social position of the church in modern, affluent societies and investigate how this position affects the church's message and method of witness.

The establishment bias of the church, as depicted on the social spectrum, results in what John Bodycomb terms the "cultural marginality of organized religion." [7] This places the church in a distinctly different position in society than that demonstrated by Jesus in the incarnation or the Anabaptists in the sixteenth century.

It is little wonder, then, that the church's message—given from position B—fails in at least two ways. It does not challenge the establishment prophetically. Nor does it catch the imagination of the marginalized, or majority A (chapter 2), as did the message of Jesus and the early Anabaptists.

From a position toward the establishment end of the spectrum, the church seeks to proclaim its message across a gaping social chasm. In spite of valiant attempts to clarify it otherwise, the church's message of the kingdom sounds similar to the establishment's message—for it seems to come from the same place. The hopeful message of the change activists of majority A has more immediate appeal to the social groupings located toward the marginalized end of the spectrum. This is because it is given from a position of social proximity.

The church tends to view the change activists of majority A as the establishment does—rabble-rousers, erratic, dangerous, a threat to social stability, "publicans and sinners." By joining the establishment in condemning this perceived threat, the church alienates the very segment of society Jesus attracted. It turns away those hungering and thirsting for righteousness, the segment potentially most receptive to the radical message of the kingdom. In so doing the church's social position is precisely that of the Pharisees, Sadducees, and Herodians. The results are devastatingly similar—misrepresentation of God and God's kingdom.

This leaves the church with the possibilities described earlier. The church's message can be one of personal salvation packaged in a way that appeals especially to the sophisticated, overstimulated, individual consumer of the establishment and majority B. The message also can be carefully advertised to appeal to individuals among the marginalized without jeopardizing the establishment values of the church in position B. The church may attempt to incorporate Christian values in a message of liberal or conservative social reform that is compatible with the establishment's agenda of reform. This also fails to attract or impact the part of society calling for more fundamental changes.

These are, of course, general observations. The church in modern, affluent societies is as pluralistic and multifaceted as are these societies themselves. There are many exceptions to these generalizations. However, it is these general tendencies, not the exceptions, which form the nonchurch public opinion about the relevance of the church. This public opinion is closer to the truth than we like to admit. It is difficut to pin the blame for negative public opinion on media bias, spiritual warfare, humanism, or anything else within or beyond society. Jesus too faced all these things.

The fact is that churches which consistently proclaim and live out the gospel message, visibly demonstrating the radical hope of the coming kingdom after the manner of Jesus and the early church, are the exception. Churches with a message counter to the tired values of the establishment in modern affluent society are rare. Churches which are in society in the way Jesus was in his are a tiny minority indeed.

Learning to Be in Mission from Position A

That brings us to this question: can the church-in-mission begin to witness in modern affluent societies in authentic ways? Is the social location of the church within modern affluent society a matter of choice? Missionaries and church planters from North America, working in modern affluent societies, are both sent *from* a society where the church exists in peaceful, impotent coexistence with the establishment and *to* societies where this is also the norm. Perhaps we are proposing an impossibility.

As part of exploring the possibilities for deliberate social location by missionaries and church planters, I surveyed five congregations established by Mennonite missionaries in London, Munich, Dublin, Hong Kong, and Tokyo.

Mennonite congregations were chosen for several reasons. First, as spiritual heirs to the Anabaptists, Mennonites can trace their roots directly to a people movement of the Spirit which began among a distinctly antiestablishment social grouping.

Second, Mennonites profess to be "strangers and pilgrims." They are "in the world but not of the world."

Finally, by comparing several models of witness within one denomination, any variation in social location could, I felt, be attributed to factors other than denominational identity.

Despite the focus here on Mennonite congregations, my hope was that applications would be broader. Any insights about choices of social location and how this affects the witness of the emerging church would, I hoped, be useful for missionaries of any denomination or tradition.

The first objective was to find, from the viewpoint of the current leader or representative, the perceived social position of each of the five churches in their societies. Also explored would be the *ideal* social position, again from the point of view of the leader or representative. Would these two be the same?

All five churches surveyed, although separated by continents and oceans, were perceived as being located within the majority on the social spectrum. This is precisely where the leaders or representatives thought they should be located. This would support the assumption that the missionaries' church will tend to be located socially where the missionary is or attempts to be.

Significantly, while all five churches were quite close together on the socioeconomic scale, there was a wide variety of attitudes about the church's social position in society, the use of power, and the nature of hope. This supports my earlier assertion that within the majority category there exists relative freedom to make diverse and even conflicting social choices.

The leaders or representatives of all five churches believed that the congregation should be located in the majority social grouping of society. All five believed the church should be integrated into society while working to change it. This suggests the possibility for the church in mission to be at once integrated into society and offer real alternatives to some of society's features. Might it be possible for the church to identify with a social grouping that is at once integrated into society *and* hoping and working for substantial social change?

Several important things became clear in the survey. First, missionaries, church planters, and leaders can influence the church's social position. In fact, the social location of the missionary seems to be the main factor determining where the church begins within society.

Second, it seems that the missionaries, church planters, or leaders clearly have an influence on which direction the church goes socially. They help determine whether it moves toward the establishment or the marginalized ends of the spectrum. The values the missionaries, church planters, or leaders communicate to the emerging church apparently become integrated into the group. These values are then eventually lived out in the form of social location.

Third, it is possible for a church to have a social position within society consistent with its message of hope in the coming kingdom. It is possible to communicate and demonstrate this message from a permanent social location leaning toward the marginalized end of the social spectrum. It is possible to live with misunderstanding and tension from the establishment and the affirmation of the social grouping of the majority A. It *is* possible. However, as the survey indicated, it is *not* easy.

So what can be concluded? Is the incarnational approach effective? Is the authenticity of the above model validated by dramatic church growth? Not necessarily in the churches examined. In fact, when looking at short-term numerical growth of a particular congregation, a social position toward the establishment end of the social spectrum appears slightly superior to other alternatives.

But that is for the short-term. Short-term numerical growth of a particular congregation, however, is not the only criterion against which effectiveness can or should be measured. It just happens to be the easiest. Other criteria can be used. They include authenticity, potential people movements of the Spirit, the social impact of the gospel, growth of the kingdom of God over a long period of time, and taking as normative the models of Jesus, the early church, and the Anabaptists. When such criteria are used, a social position oriented toward the marginalized end of the spectrum is vastly superior.

When the church in mission announces and lives out the good news of the kingdom from this deliberate social position, it is most likely to be socially in the world as Jesus was in the world. Its message and method of announcing and demonstrating the kingdom of God, developed out of this position in society, will be consistent with the example of Jesus. The church in mission may, like Jesus, suffer misunderstanding and reaction from the establishment. Like Jesus it may be almost overwhelmed—sometimes with surges of popularity, other times with mass disillusionment among the crowds looking for immediate solutions.

Witness after the model of Jesus may include the apparent failure of suffering and crucifixion. It may mean the triumph of resurrection and Pentecost, of turning the world upside down. Authentic witness to the good news of the kingdom is the life of Jesus in the world.

In the final chapter we will examine the practical aspects of carrying out the incarnational approach to missions in modern affluent societies.

CHAPTER 6

An Incarnational Approach to Mission

The Social Dimension of Authentic Witness

"As you sent me into the world," Jesus prayed, "I have sent them [the disciples] into the world" (John 17:18). When one looks at the context of this phrase in Jesus' prayer, and when one examines the entire ministry of Jesus, this seems clear: Jesus is implying that his disciples, and all witnesses to the kingdom, are to be *socially* in the world as he himself was.

Unless the church is socially in the world as Jesus was, it will be difficult, if not impossible, to communicate and demonstrate the good news of the kingdom as Jesus did. Jesus was in his world in a particular way, in a particular social location. Even a cursory examination of the Gospel of Luke, for instance, suggests that Jesus had a particular concern for all marginalized people, including the poor, women, and lepers and other outcasts.

Likewise, our authenticity in witness begins with the fundamental choice of incarnation—our social location as witnesses within society. How can we missionaries and church planters in modern affluent societies be in a social position comparable to the one Jesus chose?

As we have seen, our theology, and then our message and method of communication, is always done in the context of our social location. This is true regardless of whether or not we have deliberately chosen our social location or made a conscious effort at contextualizing the message. A brief look at contextualization in modern affluent societies may help highlight the importance of social location.

Contextualization

Contextualization in modern affluent societies is often understood superficially. It is seen as involving techniques for communicating the gospel or improving the church's "image problem" with public relations know-how. "Real" contextualization occurs when the gospel is introduced into new cultures.

This concept is a mistake. Two things need to be said about contextualization in modern affluent societies. First, the gospel is contextualized not only in those settings Western missionaries explore but also *in the missionaries' home turf*. "Contextualization," says Lesslie Newbigin, "thinks mainly of the gospel in Third World countries, ignoring the fact that contextualization of the gospel has already happened in Western culture."[1]

We have seen that the tendency for the church in Western culture is to shift socially toward the establishment end of the social spectrum. Ignoring the fact that contextualization has already occurred leads missionaries to blissfully perpetrate the very same establishment bias of the church from which they were sent and to do this in the name of mission.

Because affluent societies seem so familiar to missionaries from North America, they may conclude that contextualization in the new society is merely a process of strategic adjustment in the area of communication and persuasion. Theology is largely irrelevant.

Such views leave the establishment status quo unchallenged. They also shape the content of the message and the method of communicating the message in the same way as did the society from which the missionary was sent. Thus the unauthentic witness of the sending church will be a contextualized unauthentic witness in the new society. Contextualized unfaithfulness is not the gospel, no matter how effective the programs of the church are.

A second dynamic that is easy to overlook is that *modern societies are not a single entity*. Affluent societies, like other societies, are societies in tension and conflict. The pluralism of choices in modern affluent societies makes this inevitable. Michael Hogan, in his book on the church in Australia writes,

> It is impossible to imagine a society surviving without some conflict. Although some people find it disagreeable, many social theorists suggest that conflict and competition are necessary signs of life. In many instances the obvious rivalry is between individuals who struggle to achieve knowledge, prestige, wealth or power. Yet it is clear that in every modern state there are more organized and permanent bases of competition, rivalry and conflict.[2]

The missionary comes to a society in tension, a society where incarnational choices of social location are as inevitable and crucial as those in the time of Jesus or the early Anabaptists. Intentionally or unintentionally, the missionary joins sides within society. The church that emerges as the result of the missionary's efforts, whether it seeks to withdraw from the public arena or become actively involved in it, will exist in society as some part of the permanent bases of competition, rivalry, and conflict.

Understanding the social dimension of witness involves recognizing the establishment bias in Western contextualization of the gospel. It involves awareness that the missionary comes to a society in tension. And the missionary will inevitably identify with social groupings in conflict with one another.

In modern affluent societies, deliberately choosing the social location from which to witness is both possible and necessary to be authentic, to be in the world like Jesus was. As with Jesus, it is not the missionary's identification with society in general that will determine the nature of her witness. It is the deliberate identification with a particular grouping within society that will determine how missionaries' ministries are perceived and the impact their words have on individuals and groups. Their chosen social location will affect how missionaries communicate the good news of the kingdom. Their location will determine the appeal and the threat of the good news within society.

The incarnational approach to missions begins then with a commitment to make the basic choice of incarnation: to demonstrate and communicate the good news of the kingdom. This means contextualizing the gospel in a specific social grouping within society.

Social Location in Incarnational Mission

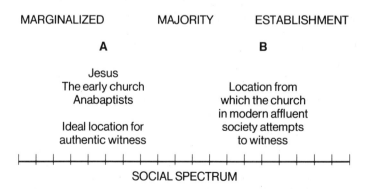

The missionary should attempt to identify, as Jesus did, with the social grouping most receptive to the good news—those hungering and thirsting for righteousness, actively seeking the kingdom of God, willing to take personal risks to participate in change. The church, as it emerges from this group, is likely to demonstrate and communicate the gospel authentically to the whole of society. This location is shown below.

Jürgen Moltmann has commented, "Mission is taking part in the messianic sending of Jesus and as such taking part in the people, with which he so much identified himself." [3] How is it possible to take part with the people with whom Jesus identified? What does this mean practically for the missionary? For the remainder of the book, we examine the possibilities for implementing the incarnational approach in missions.

Choosing the Incarnational Approach

Missionaries and church planters should not come to their new area of witness with a list of goals and a clear strategy for achieving their goals. They should come instead with a clear commitment to identify with the people most likely to receive the message of the gospel. They should intend to reach people who, as the church, will communicate and demonstrate the gospel with authenticity. Their aim should be people who can share hope with the marginalized, who will call all persons to faith, and who will prophetically challenge the social sins committed and promoted by the establishment.

Choosing social position A

The incarnational approach, in short, begins with a commitment to the priority of choosing a social location which revolves around position A.

This task calls for critical listening. There are many secular and Christian voices, often with conflicting messages, within modern affluent societies. These voices stridently clamor for the attention and support of the missionary. To which voices does the missionary listen? Which voices should inform the missionary of the needs within society and the opportunities for communicating the good news?

This critical listening, so important in choosing social location, takes time. "Missionary endeavor, and in particular that of urban industrial missions, before engaging in all programs of action and aid *for* the people should first discover Christ *in* the people."[4] The first major challenge is to spend the necessary time listening instead of plunging into the kinds of activity that impress the folks back home.

Sending churches and mission boards in modern affluent societies tend to reflect their culture's orientation toward swift, quantitative success. Most missionaries and church planters want to be successful, to live up to the expectations of their supporters. A sympathetic sending church or mission board committed to the high cost of authenticity greatly facilitates the missionary's incarnational choice.

The commitment to make incarnational choices is difficult because it is unnatural. Such a choice has probably never been made by the supporting church, mission board, or missionaries themselves. It is unlikely that the Christians missionaries meet in their new society have made incarnational choices. No one, except perhaps the missionary, is likely to understand the necessity of "wasting" time in this way. Shortcuts are sought by sending groups hoping for quick results and by missionaries hoping for quick integration, acceptance, and legitimacy.

Partnering strategies

One such shortcut is to form "partnerships" in mission. These partners can be individuals, churches, and organizations in the new society who seem to share vision similar to that of the sending group or missionary. These partners may request assistance from the sending group or may offer to cooperate in new programs.

On the surface this appears to be sound strategy. Working with partners gives an immediate "in" for missionaries and their sending groups in the new areas. It seems to offer instant credibility. It provides an opportunity for missionaries to be locally accountable in witness.

The sending group, hoping to avoid giving any impression of outside domination and patronization and sensitive to the flaws of colonial missions in the past, may confer the status of "partner" on these individuals or groups. They may begin to develop program strategy in consultation with them.

Efforts to avoid imperialism are indeed commendable. However, this partnering strategy is flawed for several reasons. For one, this is a strategic choice rather than an incarnational one. It may actually hinder careful incarnational choices to be made by the missionary. It may prevent authentic witness from occurring by committing programs prematurely to a specific direction, a direction which can then become extremely difficult to change.

The greatest flaw of partnering strategy is that those in the new society who seek partnering with the missionary and sending group may themselves be in the wrong social location for authentic witness. They may not be integrated into society at *any* point on the spectrum. They may not be accountable to anyone but themselves. They may be seeking or agreeing to partnership with an outside organization to achieve personal dreams of grandeur or to get power, recognition, or self-fulfillment. Partners may be mavericks within their own society. They may be individuals or organizations alienated from the mainstream.

The missionary too, it can be argued, may have at least

some of these traits. This is true. But the possibility of screening applicants before assigning them, as well as recalling them should such traits become obvious, prevents some harm. It is easier to detect socially isolated individuals in one's own society, for instance, than in other cultures.

The point is that making the first step "listening to the natives" by forming partnerships of convenience does not insure that the missionary will be integrated into the receptive social grouping of his new society or even integrated at all. The "natives" may say conflicting things for different reasons. The missionaries and their sending groups, like presidents of powerful countries, can usually find "natives" who are willing, even eager, to build their own power bases by cooperating with an outside organization for a time.

Besides putting the initial incarnational choice of social location at risk, premature partnering can jeopardize the process of self-theologizing of the emerging church. Contextualization begins as soon as the emerging church starts to grapple with the issues facing them in their society. The freedom for self-theologizing *must* be introduced and maintained by the missionary. This freedom may be threatened if the native partner has embraced a theological package or denominational tradition developed outside the local society.

Charles Kraft comments, "The contextualization of Christian theology is, therefore, not simply the passing on of a 'product' that has been developed once and for all in Europe or America."[5] A good missionary is trained to be sensitive to the cultural aspects of the gospel. He may thus sometimes better understand the dynamics of contextualization and have a deeper commitment to foster the process within the emerging congregation than the native partner who has chosen to identify with a foreign tradition.

Don Carrington writes,

Contextualization is not a theology but a process placing power and control in the hands of local . . . people. In case studies concerned with hermeneutics, those same indigenous people are the ones who must engage in a process of discernment for they are the "Church" in that place.[6]

To summarize, it seems that authenticity of witness—beginning with initial incarnational choices and continuing with the ongoing process of contextualization—is most likely to occur when the missionary has the time and the freedom to make incarnational choices from the beginning. Premature partnership arrangements, made for strategic reasons, put this essential freedom in jeopardy.

But what are the alternatives? Freelance missionaries, responsible to no one but themselves? A reversion to the self-assured denominational or parachurch imperialism which characterizes some mission endeavors even today?

No. The model of Jesus demonstrated in the incarnation points to a third alternative. Jesus' example shows us an incarnational alternative. There is a better way than strategic organizational relationships made prematurely with socially nonintegrated partners in a new society or denominational or parachurch imperialism. This alternative is *organic, personal relationships formed naturally and primarily with people in social grouping A by the missionary.* These relationships include both Christians and non-Christians.

Implementing the Incarnational Approach

Missionaries beginning with the incarnational approach in modern affluent society need two things. They need to be committed to identify within their new society from within social grouping A. This commitment is necessary despite the time it takes and despite other expectations that the establishment and their supporters in the new society may have. In addition, missionaries need from their sending group a policy that gives them the freedom, time, and support required for this task.

Assuming that missionaries arrive in their new society with these two essential components, how do they locate in social grouping A? Social groupings in modern affluent societies do not live in distinct suburbs into which the missionary can move. They do not advertise for membership in the Yellow Pages. Welcome Wagon does not have brochures with telephone numbers listed under "Majority A."

Integrated critics

To identify with social grouping A, the missionary must from the outset find, listen, and relate to those in the new society who could be labeled "integrated critics." Who are integrated critics? They are persons integrated socially into the mainstream of society *and at the same time* aware of and concerned about the needs and shortcomings within it.

Integrated critics are those who actively seek, promote, and engage in alternatives to the status quo. They may simply be disillusioned with the status quo. They may be motivated by utopian dreams. They may be both.

Relating to integrated critics is vital. "The first step to take," writes Jacques Ellul about the role of the Christian presence within society, "is to become aware of our world."[7] Integrated critics are already aware of both the successes and failures of the world in which they are a part. They are also likely to be aware of possibilities for change.

To be critical about society as a newly arrived missionary is common but not helpful. Modern affluent society, already has an adequate supply of negative, marginalized critics. *Integrated* critics are full participants in their society, involved in working for change. As such they can help the missionary understand, not only the problems in that society, but current responses as well. Integrated critics can help missionaries become aware of the motivating hopes of change activists.

The incarnational approach begins, then, as the missionary relates to and is informed by these integrated critics. The missionary's relationships with integrated critics could be seen as primary. The relationships with either complacent integrated persons or marginalized critics could be seen as secondary.

How are integrated critics to be identified? They are those who hunger and thirst for righteousness to the extent that they are prepared at least to protest lack of righteousness. Although concentrated around position A on the social spectrum, integrated critics in modern affluent societies may be found from one end of the socioeconomic scale to the other. They can be found in and outside the church.

The first place for the missionary to identify and listen to the integrated critic is in the existing church. This is because the gospel is already being faithfully incarnated and contextualized by at least a minority of the church in its society. Within every church tradition are prophetic, visionary voices calling for radical discipleship, the reform of oppressive structures of church and state, a commitment to the poor, and many other gospel-based ideas.

Finding the integrated critics in the church is not difficult. The missionary need only begin visiting various churches, inform himself of the various Christian organizations, and contact interest groups and theological schools. Such explorations will reveal the individuals and the networks of integrated critics that already exist in the church within the society to which the missionary has come. Signs of authenticity and hope within the church in modern affluent societies, like a light on a hill, cannot remain hidden long, even from a missionary "outsider"!

Within several months of moving to Perth, we found examples in Australia of whole networks of integrated critics.

We discovered, for instance, the Australian Network of Christian Communities, whose aim is "to present corporate challenge to the church and society."

Another example is the Australian Association for Urban Missions, whose stated purpose includes "communicating by word and deed the Good News of the kingdom in appropriate ways for the Australian setting, listening to and identifying with the poor and disadvantaged, and working prophetically for God's justice in Church and Community." Examples like these can be found in every modern affluent society.

There are several good reasons for beginning the incarnational approach to mission by identifying with the integrated critic within the existing church of the new society. First, this acknowledges those unique expressions of faithfulness of the indigenous church within its society. We missionaries and church planters have much to learn from these expressions of faithfulness present in *every* Christian tradition in *every* society.

If we are honest, we will discover this: within the church in the society to which we have come, the process of incarnational contextualization of the gospel has already been occurring at least as faithfully as in our own home church. This is a humbling revelation for those of us convinced of the superiority of our own particular tradition. But it is absolutely essential to the integrating process of the incarnational approach.

There is another good reason for identifying with the integrated critic in the existing church. It is that such identification gives missionaries a readily identifiable and reliable social grouping with whom they can join in the common task of communicating and demonstrating the gospel.

For denominational missionaries, this relationship of solidarity is immediately beneficial for both the missionary and those with whom he identifies. The denominational missionary represents a distinct historic Christian tradition. At least part of that tradition can contribute to, encourage, and enrich the indigenous expressions of faithfulness. At the same time, by identifying and joining with the integrated critics, missionaries are likely to begin to become integrated themselves in ways that challenge them to faithfully adapt their own tradition in new and relevant ways.

Finally, identifying with the Christian integrated critic will likely bring the missionary together with the integrated critic outside of the church. Within the churches in modern affluent societies, Christian visionaries and prophets often find themselves associating closely with secular ones in calling for and working together for common causes and challenging the evils of the status quo.

A deliberate choice to identify with the integrated critics in the church who in turn associate closely with secular integrated critics can be costly for the missionary. Since the time Jesus ate and drank with sinners, solidarity between visionary Christians and secular change activists continues to be misunderstood by the church, which feels its image threatened. The establishment also feels threatened by such coalitions.

Because of this bias, shared with the Pharisees and Herodians, missionaries and their sending groups tend to view close relationships with secular integrated critics as legitimate only if the intention is to proclaim the gospel to this group. But missionaries, like Jesus, must eat and drink with "sinners." Missionaries must do so to communicate the gospel and learn from "sinners." But they must also associate with "sinners" to integrate themselves into the right location in society for communicating the gospel to all of society.

"Mission," writes Jürgen Moltmann, "does not mean only proclamation, teaching, and healing, but it also involves eating and drinking. The eating and drinking mission anticipates the kingdom among the hungry and thirsty."[8]

John Smith of Australia is an ex-bikie who has become one of Australia's leading evangelists and social critics. He is an integrated critic who urges Christians to eat and drink with sinners. In his recent book, *Advance Australia Where?* he writes,

> Somehow the real Jesus should have appealed long ago to that "other half" of Australian thinkers, artists and common people whose politics were left of centre. But from the beginning, the Australian church botched the publicity and advertised a different and strangely unbiblical—sometimes unattainable—Jesus who belonged in the pasty "other world" of the cathedral's stained-glass windows. . . . If the church is to reach the people of Australia, it will be when we begin to feel something of the alienation of humanity without God. This deep sense of cosmic orphanhood has taken root in the hearts of the thinkers down through the history of this nation, yet there are few Christians able to empathize with that feeling of despair.[9]

This ability to make and maintain genuine relationships with integrated critics outside the church will help the missionary locate within society where Jesus did, be socially in the world as Jesus was, and communicate the gospel authentically within and outside of this social grouping. This is the incarnational position of vulnerability, of social tension, of misunderstanding. It is also the incarnational position of hope for those who hunger and thirst for righteousness. It is the position from which hope can be shared with the hopeless. It is the position out of which people movements grow and challenge the social sins perpetrated by the establishment.

Jesus was in this social position because of a divine choice in the incarnation. The Anabaptists were there at least partly because they chose to identify with Jesus in their society. Missionaries of all traditions are free to make the same costly choices.

Because integrated critics are socially integrated, they are relationally linked with others, especially those around social position A. This integration makes possible their participation in people movements that begin within this social grouping and may potentially impact all of society. Integrated critics are, like Peter, potential leaders of such movements.

A word of caution is necessary here. In our experience, not all integrated critics are the same. There seems to be two kinds of integrated critics, who, like the disciples of Jesus, are attracted to the witness of the kingdom at hand. First are those who, like Peter, genuinely hunger and thirst for righteousness. The hopes and dreams of these integrated critics are larger than themselves.

There is another kind of integrated critics, however. Although a minority among critics, their attraction to the kingdom seems to be, at best, as a means of self-actualization. Their hunger and thirst for righteousness is limited to their own person. These self-seeking integrated critics can easily be confused with the genuine ones, for they espouse popular causes that enhance their own personal struggles.

Judas is an example of the self-seeking integrated critic. His concern for the poor seemed genuine to the disciples and probably even to Jesus. But Judas had a hidden agenda. Just what this destructive, hidden agenda was is not clear, but Judas was willing to follow Jesus and fit into the group of disciples until it became obvious to him that Jesus and the kingdom were not meeting his expectations. At that point Judas betrayed Jesus and the other disciples.

A self-seeking integrated critic welcomed by a missionary can be destructive as Judas was. The emerging group can be seen by this person as a means of fulfilling selfish, limited objectives and personal ambitions. The emerging group is accessible. There is a chance to speak and be heard. There is affirmation. There is no elaborate system of censure. It is malleable. It is ready-made for the self-seeking integrated critic. But if the selfish and often unrealistic objectives are not fulfilled, the emerging church can readily become the target of scorn and even betrayal.

This is the risk of authentic witness. There seem to be no safeguards which prevent potentially destructive people from coming into an emerging church. It seems that Jesus' example is to call everyone while recognizing the danger signals in individuals. Authentic witness, like Jesus' witness, is never a very secure undertaking. It is vulnerable.

As discussed earlier, the gospel, incarnated and communicated from within social grouping A, has the potential, not only to confront and appeal to individuals, but to ignite a people movement of the Spirit and impact all of society. Jesus and his followers, the early church following Pentecost, and the Anabaptists are all examples we have looked at. Let us examine what all this means practically. Is it really possible to identify with integrated critics around social position A and to do so without compromising the message of the gospel?

In modern affluent societies, some integrated critics and the people they represent and inspire are to be found within the establishment. Although rare, establishment integrated critics can provide a consistent, prophetical challenge from within to the false values of the status quo.

Oregon Senator Mark Hatfield has consistently opposed the arms race. Senator Jo Vallentine of Western Australia, a Quaker who has led the way against the visits of U.S. nuclear warships to Australian waters. Both could be seen as examples of establishment integrated critics in the political sphere. There are also the prophets and visionaries within church leadership circles, such as South African Archbishop

Desmond M. Tutu. Such persons might be seen as integrated critics within the church institutional establishment.

Far more common (and more accessible to missionaries and almost everyone else!) are the integrated critics within the majority who advocate grass-roots change and work at alternate solutions in the face of the establishment's obvious failures. Examples of these include secular peace groups, environmental activists, prison reform advocates, civil rights activists, alternative school founders, and Amnesty International. These and many other similar interest groups work, often sacrificially, for social change for the benefit of others.

I have personally been deeply humbled by the selfless efforts of some German friends of ours. Agnostics motivated by a sense of justice and a vision for a better world, they spent countless hours and money helping refugees begin new lives in Germany.

It would seem a natural step for missionaries to identify with at least some of these movements within their societies and to contribute to them by active participation. This certainly *should* happen. On the level of working for peace, justice, and stewardship of creation, for instance, Christians and non-Christians share common concerns. On this level they can be drawn together. The good news shared from this common level can be good from the point of view of those looking for goodness in this world. The gospel takes on new meaning.

Is there danger of compromise in identifying too closely with nonbelievers? Is this a return to the old "social gospel" optimism? The gospel, after all, is a message of salvation from sin—including the personal sin of all individuals, not least among them change activists and integrated critics. In fact, many Christians would argue, integrated critics and change activists are more sinful than the "great silent majority" which identifies with the establishment.

What about activists' use of coercion, their manipulation

of the legal system to ram reforms into existence? What about those who advocate civil disobedience or even violence to get their opinions heard? What about rioting and looting that seems to accompany even responsible protest? What about the anti-Christian ideologies of Marxist-oriented revolutionaries? What about those agitating for changes such as abortion on demand?

Certainly it is tempting for Christians, especially missionaries and church planters trying to build up a good reputation in their new society, to distance themselves from these "publicans and sinners." It is tempting to join in the condemnation and to shout the gospel message from across this distance. It is no wonder this is tempting. Jesus himself may have been tempted to side with the Pharisees rather than with the tax collectors, to join pharisaic support of status quo righteousness and condemnation of sinners. We see his struggles with such temptation in the gospel accounts of his encounter with Satan in the wilderness.

But Jesus did not yield to the status quo. Neither should we. The fear of compromise should not prevent us from carefully relating to and identifying with the integrated critics and change activists in social position A. They are sinners. They may have wrong assumptions. They may use the wrong means, sometimes for the wrong ends.

They are also the people with whom Jesus identified. The sin of the secular change activists, including revolutionaries, should not prevent us missionaries from being identified with them. The gospel, if authentic, is as revolutionary in modern affluent societies as it was in the society of Jesus.

Ellul has commented, "The prophets of Israel always had a political part to play, which, in connection with their civilization, was genuinely revolutionary."[10] He adds, "[The Christian] guided by the Holy Spirit . . . is making an essentially revolutionary act. If the Christian is not being revolutionary, then in some way or another he has been unfaithful to his calling in the world."[11] If the fear of compromise prevents the missionary from identifying with the "publicans and sinners" around social position A, compromise of the missionary's calling has already occurred!

One of the greatest challenges facing missionaries in modern affluent societies is maintaining this close identification with sinners *and* faithful identification with Jesus and the gospel of the kingdom. Identification with publicans and sinners, as Jesus demonstrated, must not in itself mean compromise.

But compromise for missionaries in modern affluent societies is more likely to involve two possibilities other than over-identification with sinners. On one hand, we may compromise the authenticity of the gospel message if we do not identify with those around social position A as Jesus did. On the other hand, we may compromise the power of the good news by not daring to lift up Jesus and his way when identifying with them. Newbigin writes,

> World history is full of the dreams of a new order that will draw all humankind together. Every proposal for human unity that does not specify the center around which that unity is to be created . . . has the will, vision and beliefs of its creator.[12]

Thus the secular longing for the kingdom in all forms *is* to be viewed positively by the missionary in modern affluent society. But such longing must also be seen as limited and flawed. Jesus, who preached and demonstrated the good news of the kingdom from among those who ached for it, is the unifying center of humankind and history. The missionary and the church that emerges faithfully in society is a servant, witness, and sign of the kingdom.

The choice then, is not between compromise through identifying too closely with sinners on one hand, or with those who represent the "righteousness" of the status quo on the other. The choice is rather to identify with sinners *and* Jesus at the same time.

Practical ideas

Let me summarize several basic steps I have been recommending and suggest practical ideas that could help implement the incarnational approach to mission.

1. Missionaries and church planters, especially in areas where they are beginning to work, should have the freedom, time, and support necessary to implement the incarnational approach in their work.

Integration into social position A within society is the missionary's priority. The missionary can do this naturally in several ways. In Germany, for instance, when our children were old enough for school we joined a parents' initiative. Through it we helped establish an alternative Montessori school. Not only did our son have a fantastic first year in school, we learned to know non-Christian parents with concerns and interests similar to our own. Through these commonalities, authentic relationships were established, genuine friendships that have endured to the present. We invited many of these families to church events to which they eagerly came.

My wife, Janet, joined a mothers' initiative which campaigned for cleaner city playgrounds. I participated in several Christian and secular peace groups. The whole family joined secular friends and neighbors in protesting the massive buildup of medium-range nuclear weapons on German soil.

In Australia we again immediately enrolled our children in a local, parent-operated Montessori school. Within a year I began serving on its board. By working together with parents on the board and at "busy bees," we established whole new networks of satisfying friendships. Again families from the school participated in church events. Some joined the group.

My wife and I also volunteered in Christian initiatives including the Western Australian Association of Urban Missions (interdenominational), Trinity Peace Research Institute (Uniting Church of Australia), and a women's issues group (Baptist/interdenominational).

This integration, if genuine, is far more than an evangelization technique for making contacts. It allows missionaries to become integrated, to learn from integrated critics, and to contribute in legitimate ways in their new society. The missionaries are appreciated for helping out. They are put in touch with networks of relationships within both the Christian and secular communities around social position A. This gives missionaries freedom to explore the needs of the new society as well as possible responses with others who are already integrated.

A first practical step then, is to volunteer at least part-time in one or more secular or Christian organizations involved in social action.

2. The emerging faithful church should have the freedom, assistance, and support of the missionary to decide how to communicate and demonstrate the gospel within its society.

If the church has emerged from among those in social position A and includes integrated critics, whole networks of relationships already exist. The group may decide, as church, to work with the secular movements that share some common vision with the newly formed church. This can and should be done with a clear Christian identity.

In Australia, our church, after careful processing, decided to support a group of local aborigines whose ancient sacred site was being threatened by urban development. The church donated firewood for the camp where the aborigines lived. Several members joined the aborigines occupying the construction site and eventually were arrested and jailed with the aborigines.

The outcome of these activities was positive. By joining

hands with other Christians, aboriginal and white, the church was faithful in its society. A prophetic challenge to the establishment of both church and state was made without being in competition with Australian Christian expressions of faithfulness—as many imported denominational programs tended to be.

From the appreciation expressed for our support by the aborigines, both Christian and traditional, it was clear that the gospel was being communicated as good news to a people victimized by church and state for the past two hundred years. Perhaps the most important result, however, was that the church learned about the injustices toward their neighbors from their point of view.

Thus a further practical step for the emerging church is to maintain the existing organic relationships with secular social initiatives and movements which new members bring with them—and to build on them. The missionary can contribute to this process by encouraging group theological reflection and, eventually, action.

3. The goal in relating to and becoming identified with these networks and movements as Christians is to participate in a people movement of the Spirit or to contribute to the possibility of one. The goal should not merely be denominational church planting.

This is not to say that the planting and growth of denominational churches can or should be avoided. On the contrary. Mennonites will flourish as part of a people movement of the Spirit—as will Catholics, Baptists, Anglicans, and Pentecostals.

The point is that the concept of church planting and church growth, built as it often is on strategic presuppositions, seems to carry with it intrinsic competitive notions. While competition may be fine for marketing apple pie, cuckoo clocks, or boomerangs, competition is not compatible with sharing the good news of the kingdom of God. Marketing strategy, with its inherent competition, may work well in bringing people into a particular congregation. But the authenticity of the witness and the long-range effect of the gospel in its society is another question.

The Challenge of the Incarnation

"As you sent me into the world, I have sent them into the world" (John 17:18). Are we missionaries in modern affluent societies like Jesus was in his day? Are we taking the opportunities we have in witness to new areas to become like Jesus? The challenge is to respond to the call of Jesus, in spite of the difficulty and cost, and to join him where he is in the world.

Is it a fool's dream to attempt to demonstrate and preach the kingdom in modern affluent societies like Jesus did in his? Martin Leaman has written,

> The church of this fool's dream will be like its Lord. The church will become magnetic like him, and do uncommon things. Its members will have sinners as friends and yet not sin, and they will accept invitations to eat in questionable places. They will champion unsavory causes and risk tarnished reputations. They will sometimes offend multitudes by being too much like the master and too familiar with sinners. They will make the right enemies. The church will grow in numbers daily.[13]

A final look at the familiar social spectrum below showing the goals for the position and role of the emerging church in modern affluent society may be helpful in conceptualizing the possibilities mentioned in the "fool's dream" above.

The community of authentic witness, as seen above, incarnates the gospel within society in the manner of Jesus, the early church, and the Anabaptists. It does this by identi-

Social Location and Authentic Witness Today

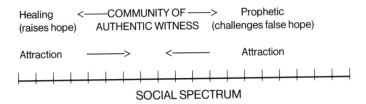

MARGINALIZED   MAJORITY   ESTABLISHMENT

A   **B**

JESUS
THE EARLY CHURCH
ANABAPTISTS

Healing   <——COMMUNITY OF——>   Prophetic
(raises hope)   AUTHENTIC WITNESS   (challenges false hope)

Attraction   ——————>   <——————   Attraction

SOCIAL SPECTRUM

fying with Jesus and with those who seek the kingdom. In doing so the community of authentic witness is in society in a way which anticipates, works for, and participates in a potential people movement of the Spirit.

From this social location, individuals are called to repentance and faith from one end of the spectrum to the other. The social impact of this call to repentance and faith coming from social position A, is not uniform across the spectrum. The gospel from this position raises the hopes of the marginalized, offers alternatives to the misplaced hopes of the majority, and challenges the false hopes of the establishment.

We who are involved in new missions endeavors in modern affluent societies are called to be and to do what Jesus calls all his followers, in every time and place, to be and to do. Jesus calls us to be in the world, announcing and demonstrating the good news of the kingdom of God as Jesus demonstrated in his life. The community of Jesus is the community of authentic witness to the extent that it identifies with

Jesus in society. From this position the community of authentic witness incarnates the gospel as Jesus did.

"As you sent me into the world," Jesus prayed, "I have sent them into the world." And so we have been *sent* by Jesus, to be like him in our world. It is up to us to *be* like him. Let us take up the challenge of the incarnation in the choices we make in mission. Let us be like Jesus in the world!

Study Questions

Chapter 1

1. Try to identify features of secularism which are obivous in your community. Does secularism affect your church's efforts to witness in your community? What are the negative effects of secularization on your church's witness? The positive effects?

2. Is strategic thinking by the church a modern phenomenon? Discuss the pros and cons of such thinking.

3. What are some ways market-based approaches have produced positive results for churches in your community? What have been some negative results?

4. Have you or your church consciously selected target groups to whom you direct your efforts of witness? If so, attempt to identify ways this has affected the method and message of your church.

Chapter 2

1. With the social spectrum in front of you or your group, test the categories of marginalization, power, and hope against your own experience of your community and society. Does the social spectrum represent your community? Who are the marginalized? What persons represent the establishment?

2. Do you think the social location of Jesus in the incarnation was a deliberate choice? Why or why not?

3. Pluralism and secularism offer more possibilities for choosing social location than ever before. Do you agree? What determines your own choices?

4. Think about your own position on the social spectrum in relation to Jesus' position.

Chapter 3

1. Discuss the idea that the social location of Jesus was a key feature of the incarnation. Do you think Jesus could have moved toward a social location different from the one in which he was born? How do you think this would have changed the impact of his message on his society?

2. In the Gospels, look at Jesus' encounters with people such as Zacchaeus, Nicodemus, and the Samaritan woman. Note the comments from observers. How does the social spectrum help interpret the actions and reactions of the people in the stories?

3. Discuss the advantages of Jesus' preaching the good news of the kingdom from social position A. Were there disadvantages?

4. Do you agree that the early church began in the same social location as Jesus did? What effect did this have on society in general? On the authorities? Did the church remain in this social location? What happened?

Chapter 4

1. Discuss possible reasons why the early Anabaptists were viewed as dangerous by the Reformers—even though they shared many theological assumptions.

2. Discuss the assertion that the Anabaptists' message was shaped in part by the larger social movement of the Peasants' War. Can you think of modern equivalents to this phenomenon?

3. If Hans Hut were alive today, would you invite him to speak in your church? Discuss why he would or would not be welcome.

Chapter 5

1. Do you think it is possible for the church to maintain a position at social location A? What makes it so difficult?

2. What are the risks for a church which attempts to operate out of social location A?

3. Try to locate your own church on the social spectrum. Do you think it is at the same social location in your community as when it started? Why or why not?

4. Do you think your church is at the right place on the social spectrum? Why or why not?

Chapter 6

1. Discuss this assertion: "Unless the church is socially in the world as Jesus was, it will be difficult, if not impossible, to communicate and demonstrate the good news of the kingdom as Jesus did."

2. Do you think that, in modern society, suffering is the inevitable result of being in the world as Jesus was? Why or why not?

3. What could be the equivalent to Jesus' eating and drinking with sinners for your church in your community?

4. Who are those who hunger and thirst for righteousness in your community? How do you and your church relate to them?

5. Discuss the possibilities of the incarnational approach for your church.

Notes

Introduction

1. Jürgen Moltmann, *The Power of the Powerless* (London: SCM Press, Ltd., 1983), p. 35.

Chapter 1

1. The gathering of Anabaptist leaders who met to discuss, among other things, the directions each would go in spreading the gospel in Europe, became known as the Martyrs' Synod because many of the participants suffered death following the conference.

2. Sources: *World Christian Encyclopedia*, David C. Barrett, ed. (New York: Oxford University Press, 1982). Also *The United States and World Development: Agenda 1980*, Martin M. McLaughlin and the Staff of the Overseas Development Council (New York: Praeger Publishers, 1980).

3. Bruce Wilson, *Can God Survive in Australia?* (Sutherland: Albatross, 1983), p. 35.

4. Lesslie Newbigin, *Foolishness to the Greeks: The Gospel and Western Culture* (London: SPCK, 1986), p. 20.

5. Orlando Costas, *Is There Hope in the City?* (Philadelphia: Westminster Press, 1977), p. iii.

6. For an investigation of those ideologies and values with which the message of the gospel comes into conflict in modern affluent societies, the works of Bruce Wilson of Australia, *Can God Survive in Australia?* (Sutherland, Australia: Albatross, 1983); Jacques Ellul of France, *The Meaning of the City*, trans. Denis Pardee (Nashville, Tenn.: Abingdon, 1970), and Lesslie Newbigin of En-

gland, *Foolishness to the Greeks* (London: SPCK, 1986), are all to be recommended.

7. Peter Berger, in his book *The Sacred Canopy* (Garden City, N.Y.: Doubleday, 1979), details the role of religion in facilitating and legitimizing the achievements of human society in its nationalistic self-interests.

8. Roger Greenway, ed. *Discipling the City* (Grand Rapids, Mich.: Baker Book House, 1979), p. 9.

9. In order to use inclusive language and to avoid grammatical clumsiness when referring to the missionary, the pronouns *he/him* and *she/her* will be used in separate chapters.

10. David Millikan, *The Sunburnt Soul: Christianity in Search of an Australian Identity* (Homebush West Australia: Anzea Publishers, 1981), p. 48.

11. The faulty reasoning of this kind of argument is pointed out by John Howard Yoder in "Church Growth Issues in Theological Perspective," *The Challenge of Church Growth*, ed. Wilbert R. Shenk, (Scottdale, Pa.: Herald Press, 1973), p. 30.

12. Donald R. McGavran, *Understanding Church Growth*, (Grand Rapids, Mich.: William B. Eerdmans Publishing Company, 1980), p. 265.

13. John Howard Yoder, "Church Growth Issues in Theological Perspective," in *The Challenge of Church Growth*, p. 27.

14. Newbigin, *Foolishness to the Greeks*, p. 16.

15. Roelf Kuitse, "Neo-Paganism," *Mission Focus* 16 (September 1988): 43.

16. Paul Hiebert, "Window Shopping for the Gospel," *Urban Mission* (May 1987): 5-12.

17. David Sheppard, in his book *Bias to the Poor* (London: Hodder and Stoughton, 1982), devotes an entire chapter (11) to attitudes toward the poor. In popular thinking in Britain, for example, the three most common causes for poverty are seen to be laziness, chronic unemployment, and drink.

18. Wilson, *Can God Survive?* pp. 134-135.

19. This dilemma is readily recognized by both missionaries and missiologists. An Australian missions sociologist, Peter Kaldor, in his book *Who Goes Where? Who Doesn't Care?* (Homebush West, Australia: Lancer, 1987), describes the social distance between the church in Australia and the obviously needy it seeks to reach. He writes: "The way churches organize and express themselves today is likely to be more attractive to those with higher social status. . . ." (p. 131).

20. Lausanne Committee for World Evangelism, "Christian Witness to the Urban Poor," *Lausanne Occasional Papers*, No. 22 Thailand Report, p. 14.

21. Ibid., p. 14.

22. Wilson, *Can God Survive?* p. 102.

23. Ibid., p. 95.

24. Stuart Fowler, "The Willing Captive," *Interchange* 32 (1983): pp. 54-55.

25. Ibid., p. 55.

26. Ibid., p. 57.

27. Peter Kaldor "Moving Forward in the City," *Zadok Centre Series* No. 2, Paper T 18, p. 7.

28. The concept of authenticity in witness is the theme of C. Norman Kraus's book *The Authentic Witness* (Grand Rapids, Mich.: William B. Eerdmans Publishing Company, 1979). Kraus summarizes authenticity as "correspondence to an original. In this case Jesus Christ is the Original Witness. . . . He continues to be the authoritative exemplar or prototype for the church's life and witness to the gospel. . . . We are not concerned with literal imitation, but with a sharing of his style and mission" (p. 24).

Chapter 2
1. The distinction between the strategic approach described in the last chapter and the incarnational approach to which we now turn may not be immediately obvious. The question may be asked at this point whether the incarnational approach is not merely an additional element, a revision of a strategic approach, expanded to include the preliminary step of choosing or becoming aware of one's social position, then building a corresponding strategy.

As we shall see, the two approaches differ, not only at the starting point, but in both the strategy developed and in the long-term results. The main distinction between the two approaches at the starting point is that the strategic approach tends to be motivated by effectiveness in its mission endeavor while the incarnational approach is motivated by faithfulness to the mission model of Jesus.

The difference in the strategy which develops is that with the incarnational approach, the strategies emerge after the choice of social position is made. With the strategic approach, it is the social position itself which is likely to be determined on the basis of an existing strategy.

Finally, the long-term results are likely to differ. The incarnational approach which begins with a commitment to faithfulness has a good chance of resulting in a church which faithfully carries out Jesus' mission. The strategic approach, on the other hand, committed to effectiveness, has a good chance of resulting in a church effective in carrying out its own limited mission.

2. John 4:35b.

3. McGavran, *Understanding Church Growth*, p. 185.

4. Ibid., pp. 169-170.

5. Ibid., p. 273.

6. Robert L. Ramseyer, in "Anthropological Perspectives in Church Growth Theory," *The Challenge of Church Growth*, p. 73.

7. Ideas for this model come from a variety of sources which include Peter Berger's book *The Heretical Imperative* (Garden City, N.Y.: Anchor Books, 1980), in which he describes the contrasts between premodern and modern opportunities for choice in how one thinks. "Modernity," he writes, "creates a new situation in which picking and choosing becomes an imperative" (p. 25).

8. Much theological material has been written about hope. Allan W. Loy in his essay "Australian Culture—An Attempt at Theological Penetration," (*Interchange* 25, pp. 5-21) asserts that "it is hope that makes us human" (p. 8). He bases this on the works of E. Bloch (*Das Prinzip Hoffnung*) and Jürgen Moltmann (*Theology of Hope*). Loy makes a connection between hope and social change. He writes: "Static 'reality' means imprisonment; where there is no effective hope we are locked into the present moment" (p. 14).

9. Jarrel Waskom Pickett, *Christian Mass Movements in India* (Lucknow, India: Lucknow Publishing House: 1933), p. 168.

10. Gerd Theissen, in his book *Sociology of Early Palestinian Christianity*, trans. John Bowden (Philadelphia: Fortress Press, 1978), refers consistently to the "social movement" characteristic of Jesus' witness. (The original German title of the book, *Soziologie der Jesus-Bewegung* [the sociology of the Jesus-movement], emphasizes the centrality of Theissen's descriptive concept. Theissen comments: "The Jesus movement emerged out of a deep-seated crisis in Palestinian Jewish society . . . ." (p. 97).

Chapter 3

1. *Lausanne Occasional Papers*, op. cit., p. 9.

2. Ibid.

3. Both the terms *sinners* and *righteous* are also used in the conventional ways by Jesus. It seems that Jesus, when using these terms to indicate social groupings, is challenging the social attitudes of the status quo. To use *sinner* positively challenges the so-

cial attitude of the *righteous*. The term *righteous*, when used to indicate a social grouping, is used in an almost satirical way, and can be understood to mean so-called righteous or self-righteous.

4. The difficulty of attempting to construct a model of society at the time of Jesus and the early church is clearly described by Wayne A. Meeks in his study *The First Urban Christians: The Social World of the Apostle Paul*, (New Haven, Conn.: Yale University Press, 1983), pp. 51-73. To attempt to locate Jesus and the various Jewish groups on the social spectrum could be seen as a highly speculative exercise were it not for the narrow focus on the criteria of marginality, hope, and power.

5. The stories of the rich young ruler (Matthew 19:16-23) and the rich man and Lazarus (Luke 16:19-31) indicate the social distance of the rich from Jesus and the kingdom. The account of Zacchaeus (Luke 19:1-10) can be seen as an exception, for although Zacchaeus was wealthy, he had the social status of sinner and was therefore marginalized into social isolation. This points out that wealth alone did not necessarily put one in the establishment category in Jesus' time, just as it does not today.

6. Anthony J. Saldarini "The Social Class of the Pharisees in Mark," in *The Social World of Formative Christianity and Judaism*, eds. Jacob Neusner, Peder Borgen, Ernest Frerichs, and Richard Horsley (Philadelphia: Fortress Press, 1988), p. 74.

Mark Borg in *Jesus—A New Vision*, (San Francisco: Harper & Row Publishers, 1987) observes that the power of the Pharisees was their influence on the priests ("They would give their tithes only to the priests who followed Pharisaic rules of purity.") and on their use of social ostracism, (p. 89).

7. John Howard Yoder, *The Original Revolution*, (Scottdale, Pa.: Herald Press, 1971), p. 22.

8. Jürgen Moltmann, *The Open Church* (London: SCM Press Ltd., 1978), p. 103.

9. E. Stanley Jones, *Christ and Communism*, (London: Hodder and Stoughton Limited, 1935), p. 282.

10. Thiessen, *Sociology of Early Palestinian Christianity*, p. 97.

11. Albert Nolan, *Jesus Before Christianity: The Gospel and Liberation* (London: Darton, Longman and Todd Ltd., 1976), p. 65.

Chapter 4
1. Quoted by Harold S. Bender in *The Recovery of the Anabaptist Vision*, ed. Guy F. Hershberger (Scottdale, Pa: Herald Press, 1957), p. 31.

2. Hans Kasdorf, "The Anabaptist Approach to Mission," in *Anabaptism and Mission,* ed. Wilbert R. Shenk (Scottdale, Pa.: Herald Press, 1984), p. 61.

3. *Mennonite Encyclopedia* (Scottdale, Pa.: Herald Press, 1990), "Peasants' War," 5:687-688.

4. James Stayer, "Anabaptists and Future Anabaptists in the Peasants' War," *The Mennonite Quarterly Review,* LXII (April 1988): 113.

5. James Stayer, *The Anabaptists and Thomas Müntzer,* ed. James M. Stayer and Werner O. Packull (Dubuque, Iowa: Kendall/Hunt Pub. 1980), p. 1.

6. Claus Peter Clasen, *Anabaptism: A Social History 1525-1618: Switzerland, Austria, Moravia, South and Central Germany* (Ithaca, N.Y.: Cornell University Press, 1972). Stayer observes, "One is struck by the ingeniousness with which Clasen first argues . . . that there is no evidence for a link between the peasant uprising and Anabaptism, immediately after which . . . he produces evidence of such a link. It seems as though his stress on quantitative method and his eagerness to differ with the Marxists get in the way of the 'common sense' he values so much in other respects" (Stayer, "Anabaptists and Future Anabaptists," op. cit., p. 132).

7. Stayer, "Anabaptists and Future Anabaptists," op. cit., p. 99.

8. John Driver and Samuel Escobar, *Christian Mission and Social Justice* (Scottdale, Pa: Herald Press, 1978), p. 87.

9. Ibid., pp. 88-89.

10. Stayer, "Anabaptists and Future Anabaptists," op. cit., p. 102. In this article Stayer documents fresh evidence linking additional Anabaptist leaders from the beginning of the movement with the peasants' unrest.

11. Hans Hut in *Glaubenszeugnisse Oberdeutscher Taufgesinnter,* ed. Lydia Müller (Leipzig, 1938), p. 13. (My translation.)

12. For an extensive examination of the relationship between Anabaptism and humanism, see Robert S. Kreider's article, "Anabaptism and Humanism, An Inquiry into the Relationship of Humanism to the Evangelical Anabaptists." *The Mennonite Quarterly Review* 26 (April 1952): 123-141.

13. Gerhard Zschäbitz, "The Position of Anabaptism on the Continuum of the Early Bourgeois Revolution in Germany," in *The Anabaptists and Thomas Müntzer,* pp. 28-29.

14. Clasen, *Anabaptism: A Social History,* op. cit., p. 426.

15. Zschäbitz writes, "Early Anabaptism became the collective reservoir of the manifold oppositional, radical and revolutionary

responses to the revolution that had failed. . . . In it the spearhead of the anti-feudal opposition took concrete form after the Peasants' War. Its ideology was adapted to the diffuse and contradictory level of comprehension of the broad masses." In *The Anabaptists and Thomas Müntzer*, p. 32.

16. Clasen disagrees sharply with Zschäbitz and the belief that the ideas and the spirit of the rebellious peasants lived on in the Anabaptist movement. He dismisses this: "The evidence . . . does not show a link between the peasant uprising and the Anabaptist movement" (*Anabaptism: A Social History*, p. 35).

17. *Mennonite Encyclopedia*, (Scottdale, Pa.: Herald Press, 1990), "Hans Hut," 2:846-850.

18. Herbert Klassen, "The Life and Teachings of Hans Hut," *The Mennonite Quarterly Review* no. 33 (July 1959), p. 189.

19. Martin Haas, "The Path of the Anabaptists into Separation: The Interdependence of Theology and Social Behavior," in *The Anabaptists and Thomas Müntzer*, pp. 74-75.

20. Clasen, *Anabaptism: A Social History*, p. 425.

21. Gottfried Seebass, "Peasants' War" and "Anabaptism in Franconia," in *The Anabaptists and Thomas Müntzer*, p. 157.

22. Clasen, *Anabaptism: A Social History*, p. 425.

23. Ibid.

24. Wolfgang Schäufele, *Das missionarische Bewusstsein und Wirken der Täufer*, (Neukirchen-Vluyn: Neukirchener Verlag des Erziehungsvereins, 1966), p. 108. (My translation.)

25. Clasen, *Anabaptism: A Social History*, p. 154.

26. Zschäbitz, in *The Anabaptists and Thomas Müntzer*, p. 30.

27. Roland Bainton, "The Left Wing of the Reformation," in *The Anabaptists and Thomas Müntzer*, p. 44.

28. Ibid., p. 44.

29. This distance between the Anabaptist missionaries and the revolutionaries could be compared to the distance between Jesus and the Zealots. It is understandable that the revolutionaries probably missed the distinctions between judgment and revolution in the eschatological message of both Jesus and the Anabaptists.

30. John Howard Yoder, *The Original Revolution: Essays on Christian Pacifism*, (Scottdale, Pa.: Herald Press, 1977), p. 18.

31. A term used by John Howard Yoder in *The Original Revolution*, p. 18.

Chapter 5
1. Desroche's analysis is described by Wilbert Shenk in *Anabaptism and Mission*, p. 222-223.

2. Lesslie Newbigin, *Foolishness to the Greeks*, p. 102.

3. Jürgen Moltmann, *The Open Church,* p. 47.

4. Lesslie Newbigin, *Foolishness to the Greeks*, p. 109.

5. Fowler, "The Willing Captive," pp. 55-56.

6. *Lausanne Occasional Papers,* op. cit., p. 14.

7. John F. Bodycomb, "Toward Scenarios for the Church in Australia," *Colloquim,* 13 (October 1980): 8.

Chapter 6

1. Lesslie Newbigin, *Foolishness to the Greeks*, p. 3.

2. Michael Hogan, *The Sectarian Strand: Religion in Australian History* (Ringwood, N.J.: Penguin Books, 1987), p. 4.

3. Jürgen Moltmann, *The Power of the Powerless*, p. 110.

4. Ibid., p. 105.

5. Charles H. Kraft, "The Contextualization of Theology," *Evangelical Missions Quarterly* 14 (1978): 33.

6. Don Carrington, "Theologians Struggling to Cope at the End of an Era," in *The Cultured Pearl: Australian Readings in Cross-Cultural Theology and Mission,* ed. Jim Houston (Melbourne, Australia: The Joint Board of Christian Education, 1988), p. 20.

7. Jacques Ellul, *The Presence of the Kingdom,* trans. Olive Wyon (New York: Seabury Press, 1948), p. 60.

8. Jürgen Moltmann, *The Open Church*, p. 107.

9. John Smith, *Advance Australia Where?* (Homebush West, Australia: Anzea Publishers, 1988), pp. 36-37.

10. Jacques Ellul, *The Presence of the Kingdom*, p. 50.

11. Ibid., p. 49.

12. Lesslie Newbigin, *Foolishness to the Greeks*, p. 123.

13. Martin W. Lehman, "A Fool Dreams of the Future," *Gospel Herald* 82 (January 1989): 2.

Bibliography

Bainton, Roland. "The Left Wing of the Reformation." In *The Anabaptists and Thomas Müntzer*, pp. 41-45. Eds. James Stayer and Werner O. Packull. Dubuque, Iowa: Kendall/Hunt Publishers, 1980.

Barrett, David C., ed. *World Christian Encyclopedia*. New York: Oxford University Press, 1982.

Berger, Peter. *The Heretical Imperative*. Garden City, N.Y.: Anchor Books, 1980.

_____. *The Sacred Canopy*. Garden City, N.Y.: Doubleday, 1979.

Bodycomb, John F. "Toward Scenarios for the Church in Australia." *Colloquim* 13 (October 1980): p. 515.

Borg, Marcus. *Jesus—A New Vision*. San Francisco: Harper & Row Publishers, 1987.

Carrington, Don. "Theologians Struggling to Cope at the End of an Era." In *The Cultured Pearl: Australian Readings in Cross-Cultural Theology and Mission*, pp. 12-27. Ed. Jim Houston. Melbourne, Australia: The Joint Board of Christian Education, 1988.

Clasen, Claus Peter. *Anabaptism: A Social History 1525-1618:*

Switzerland, Austria, Moravia, South and Central Germany. Ithaca, N.Y.: Cornell University Press, 1972.

Costas, Orlando. *Is There Hope in the City?* Philadelphia: Westminister Press, 1987.

Driver, John and Escobar, Samuel. *Christian Mission and Social Justice.* Scottdale, Pa.: Herald Press, 1978.

Ellul, Jacques. *The Meaning of the City.* Trans. Denis Pardee. Nashville, Tenn.: Abingdon Press, 1970.

_____. *The Presence of the Kingdom.* Trans. Olive Wyon. New York: Seabury Press, 1948.

Fowler, Stuart. "The Willing Captive." *Interchange* 32 (1983): 54-61.

Greenway, Roger, ed. *Discipling the City.* Grand Rapids: Baker Book House, 1979.

Haas, Martin. "The Path of the Anabaptists into Separation: The Interdependance of Theology and Social Behavior." In *The Anabaptists and Thomas Müntzer,* pp. 72-84. Eds. James Stayer and Werner O. Packull. Dubuque, Iowa: Kendall/Hunt Publishers, 1980.

Hershberger, Guy F., ed. *The Recovery of the Anabaptist Vision.* Scottdale, Pa.: Herald Press, 1957.

Heibert, Paul. "Window Shopping for the Gospel." *Urban Mission* (May 1987): 5-12.

Hogan, Michael. *The Sectarian Strand: Religion in Australian History.* Ringwood, N.J.: Penguin Books, 1987.

Jones, E. Stanley. *Christ and Communism.* London: Hodder and Stoughton Limited, 1935.

Kaldor, Peter. *Who Goes Where? Who Doesn't Care?* Homebush West, Australia: Lancer, 1987.

_____. "Moving Forward in the City." *Zadok Centre Series* Paper T 18.

Kasdorf, Hans. "The Anabaptist Approach to Mission." In

Anabaptism and Mission, pp. 51-69. Ed. Wilbert R. Shenk. Scottdale, Pa.: Herald Press, 1984.

Klassen, Herbert. "The Life and Teachings of Hans Hut." *The Mennonite Quarterly Review* 33 (July 1959): 171-205.

Kraft, Charles H. "The Contexualization of Theology." *Evangelical Missions Quarterly* 14 (January 1978): 31-36.

Kraus, C. Norman. *The Authentic Witness*. Grand Rapids, Mich.: William B. Eerdmans Publishing Company, 1979.

Kreider, Robert S. "Anabaptism and Humanism: An Inquiry into the Relationship of Humanism to the Evangelical Anabaptists." *The Mennonite Quarterly Review* 26 (April 1952): 123-141.

Kuitse, Roelf. "Neo-Paganism." *Mission Focus* 16 (September 1988): 41-43.

Lausanne Committee for World Evangelism. "Christian Witness to the Urban Poor." *Lausanne Occasional Papers* No. 22 Thailand Report.

Lehman, Martin W. "A Fool Dreams of the Future." *Gospel Herald* 82 (January 1989): 1-3.

Loy, Allan W. "Australian Culture—An Attempt at Theological Penetration." *Interchange* 25 (1979): 5-21.

McGavran, Donald R. *Understanding Church Growth*. Grand Rapids, Mich.: William B. Eerdmans Publishing Company, 1980.

Meeks, Wayne A. *The First Urban Christians: The Social World of the Apostle Paul*. New Haven, Conn.: Yale University Press, 1983.

Mennonite Encyclopedia. Scottdale, Pa.: Herald Press, 1956. "Hut, Hans," 2:846-850.

Mennonite Encyclopedia. Scottdale, Pa.: Herald Press, 1990. "Peasants' War," 5:687-688.

Millikan, David. *The Sunburnt Soul: Christianity in Search of an*

Australian Identity. Homebush West, Australia: Anzea Publishers, 1979.

Moltmann, Jürgen. *The Power of the Powerless.* London: SCM Press Limited, 1983.

_____. *The Open Church.* London: SCM Press Ltd., 1978.

Müller, Lydia. ed. *Glaubenszeugnisse Oberdeutscher Taufgesinnter.* Leipzig, Germany: 1938.

Newbigin, Lesslie. *Foolishness to the Greeks: The Gospel and Western Culture.* London: SPCK, 1986.

Nolan, Albert. *Jesus Before Christianity: The Gospel and Liberation.* London: Darton, Longman and Todd Limited, 1976.

Pickett, Jarrel Waskom. *Christian Mass Movements in India.* Lucknow, India: Lucknow Publishing House, 1933.

Ramseyer, Robert. "Anthropological Perspectives on Church Growth Theory." In *The Challenge of Church Growth,* pp. 65-77. Ed. Wilbert R. Shenk. Scottdale, Pa.: Herald Press, 1973.

Saldarini, Anthony J., "The Social Class of the Pharisees in Mark." In *The Social World of Formative Christianity and Judaism,* pp. 69-77. Eds. Jacob Neusner, Peder Borgen, Ernest Frerichs, and Richard Horsley. Philadelphia: Fortress Press, 1988.

Schaüfele, Wolfgang. *Das missionarische Bewusstsein und Wirken der Taüfer.* Neukirchen-Vluyn: Neukirchener Verlag des Erziehungsvereins, 1966.

Seebass, Gottfried. "Peasants' War and Anabaptism in Franconia." In *The Anabaptists and Thomas Müntzer,* pp. 154-163. Eds. James Stayer and Werner O. Packull. Dubuque, Iowa: Kendall/Hunt Publishers, 1980.

Shenk, Wilbert R., ed. *Anabaptism and Mission.* Scottdale, Pa.: Herald Press, 1984.

Sheppard, David. *Bias to the Poor*. London: Hodder and Stoughton, 1982.

Smith, John. *Advance Australia Where?* Homebush West, Australia: Anzea Publishers, 1988.

Stayer, James. "Anabaptists and Future Anabaptists in the Peasants' War." *The Mennonite Quarterly Review* LXII (April 1988): 99-139.

Stayer, James and Packull, Werner O., eds. *The Anabaptists and Thomas Müntzer*. Dubuque, Iowa: Kendall/Hunt Pub., 1980.

Theissen, Gerd. *Sociology of Early Palestinian Christianity*. Trans. John Bowden. Philadelphia: Fortress Press, 1978.

Wilson, Bruce. *Can God Survive in Australia?* Sutherland, Australia: Albatross, 1983.

Yoder, John Howard. *The Original Revolution*. Scottdale, Pa.: Herald Press, 1971.

_____. "Church Growth Issues in Theological Perspective." In *The Challenge of Church Growth*, pp. 25-47. Ed. Wilbert R. Shenk. Scottdale, Pa.: Herald Press, 1973.

Zschäbitz, Gerhard. "The Position of Anabaptism on the Continuum of the Early Bourgeois Revolution in Germany." In *The Anabaptists and Thomas Müntzer*, pp. 28-32. Eds. James Stayer and Werner O. Packull. Dubuque, Iowa: Kendall/Hunt Publishers, 1980.

The Author

Linford Stutzman was born in Oregon in 1950. His father, Willard, was pastor of a Mennonite community church in the logging settlement of Cascadia. When Linford was sixteen, his family moved to the remote interior of British Columbia, Canada. There his parents were involved in mission with Native Americans, and Linford lived with them until heading south at age nineteen to begin college.

Linford was married in 1972 to Janet Scheffel. Several months after their wedding, they traveled to Israel. They lived there for almost a year, working as Christian volunteers in Jerusalem and as farm laborers on a kibbutz in Galilee.

Linford was licensed as a minister in the Lyndon congregation, Lancaster (Pa.) in 1976 and ordained for overseas ministry in 1977. From 1978-1986, Linford and Janet served with Eastern Mennonite Board in Munich, Germany, establishing an inner-city congregation in cooperation with Mennonite Home Mission. Their sons, David and Jonathan, were born in Germany.

After Munich the Stutzmans took another assignment with Eastern Mennonite Board, this time in Perth, Western Australia. There they were involved in church development. Linford helped organize and served on the executive committee of the Western Australian Association for Urban Mission, an interdenominational network of ministry to the inner city.

After four years in Australia, the Stutzmans returned to the United States and settled in Harrisonburg, Virginia, where they currently live. Having attended and graduated from Eastern Mennonite College (1984) and Seminary (1991) during intervals in their mission work, Harrisonburg was "home" for Linford and his family.

Linford is currently pursuing doctoral studies in religion and culture at the Catholic University, Washington, D.C. The Stutzmans attend Immanuel Mennonite Church, a church established in early 1992 with a vision for mission in the disadvantaged section of Harrisonburg.